MYSTERIES OF THE WORLD

Other Books by Daniel Cohen

MYSTERIES OF THE WORLD

Daniel Cohen

Doubleday & Company, Inc.
Garden City, New York

Library of Congress Cataloging in Publication Data

Cohen, Daniel.
Mysteries of the World.

Bibliography: p. 117.
Includes index.
SUMMARY: Describes 10 lesser known unexplained
and mysterious happenings in the world.
1. Curiosities and wonders—Juvenile literature.
[1. Curiosities and wonders] I. Title.
AG243.C576   001.9′4
ISBN: 0-385-13324-3 Trade
0-385-13325-1 Prebound
Library of Congress Catalog Card Number 77–82935

9 8 7 6 5 4 3

To Cleopatra and Indigo

CONTENTS

PREFACE

All right, mystery lovers, here are ten true-life puzzles to stretch your minds and tickle your imaginations. I love this kind of mystery, and you must too, or you would never have opened this book.

There are hundreds of odd, unexplained, and mysterious happenings in the world. From that vast collection of possible puzzles I have chosen ten that have particularly intrigued me. The selection is entirely a personal one.

Some mysteries you will not find in the following pages. You will not find the mystery of who built the Great Pyramid, or what happens in the Bermuda Triangle. Bigfoot, the Loch Ness monster, Atlantis, and UFOs are mentioned, but only briefly and in relation to other subjects.

The reason for omitting these extremely popular mysteries is simple. They have often been written about before, perhaps too often. The mysteries presented in this book are, if not precisely new, at least not nearly so well known.

That they are less well known, however, does not mean that the mysteries are not as good. They are, and some of them are considerably better than the more famous mysteries of today. Several of these subjects were once extremely popular but have, for no obvious reason, fallen out of fashion. Others have been well known in different parts of the world but have never caught on in America.

There is one word that you should know before starting this book—*Fortean*. If you have never heard it before and want to look it up, you probably won't find it in your dictionary. It will undoubtedly appear in future dictionaries, for it is becoming more widely used. The word comes from the name Charles Hoy Fort, an American writer who lived from 1874 to 1932. Fort loved to collect odd bits of information about strange things seen in the sky, or strange creatures reported in the sea, or about people who suddenly appeared or disappeared. Practically anything that didn't make sense in terms of the ordinary way of looking at the world was likely to find its way into Fort's files and ultimately into one of his books.

In Fort's lifetime he gathered a small band of admirers. After his death they continued his work of collecting odd bits of information. Today there are

US ISSN 0019-0144

$1.50

THE *info* JOURNAL   science AND THE unknown

the International Fortean Organization

CHARLES HOY FORT 1874 - 1932

"one measures a circle begining anywhere."

Vol.IV, No.1
Whole No. 13
May 1974

A modern Fortean
journal.

several organizations that bear the name Fortean. Practically any odd or inexplicable event is called a Fortean phenomenon. All of the mysteries in this book could be called Fortean. Much of the information was either collected originally by Charles Fort or has appeared at one time or another in the journals of Fortean organizations or the writings of other Forteans.

Most Forteans are convinced that the world is not as it seems to be, or as scientists tell us it is. They think that scientists blindly refuse to accept anything that they cannot explain in terms of their own theories. For this reason I am not truly a Fortean, though I have a deep interest in the odd and unexplained. I think that scientists have done an extremely good job at explaining how the world operates. Of course they can't answer all of the questions—nobody can. But they are not the dogmatic, narrow-minded intellectual tyrants that Charles Fort and his followers insist they are.

While scientists may indeed tend to reject some odd events a bit too quickly, Forteans are far too quick in accepting them as genuine. Often they don't even bother to inquire adequately whether a thing happened at all, before proclaiming it as a "mystery" and challenging science to explain it. In clinging to their mysteries and rejecting explanations Forteans can be the most dogmatic people around. This is particularly irritating in a group that proclaims itself the enemy of all dogma.

That is the unpleasant side of Forteanism. But there is a better side. Forteans have not lost their sense of wonder and of fun. Instead of simply slogging along and accepting what people tell them and not thinking very much about the world, Forteans are always asking all sorts of questions. Often the questions are not too good and the answers they come up with are outrageously silly, but they are better than no questions at all.

So it is in a spirit of neo-Fortean revisionism that I present these ten mysteries of the world.

MYSTERIES OF THE WORLD

1

THE GREAT
SIBERIAN EXPLOSION

I'm going to start with a dogmatic statement. The best natural mystery in the world is, what caused a gigantic explosion in Siberia back in 1908.

Now, making dogmatic statements about mysteries of the world is a dangerous and doubtful activity. The field is full of prickly characters and someone is almost sure to argue with you. I might get some argument about the Siberian explosion being the *best* mystery, but I don't think that anyone would argue very vigorously. In any list of mysteries of the world the Great Siberian Explosion would be at or near the top.

It is a subject upon which both orthodox and unorthodox thinkers agree, if not on the solution to the mystery, at least on the fact that it is a mystery.

1

Here are the basic facts of the case. At 7:17 A.M. of June 30, 1908, something from space slammed into an incredibly remote area of Siberia and exploded. The blast created a "pillar of fire" which was visible for hundreds of miles. The noise of the blast could be heard five hundred miles away. At a small village forty miles from the site of the impact, residents felt the heat of the blast, and the shock waves it created tore up sod, broke windows, and tossed people about.

The population center nearest the blast site was Kansk, a stop on the newly created Trans-Siberian railway. It is 375 miles away from the center of the explosion, and yet even there the blast rattled windows and shook people off roofs. A train heading for Kansk was practically shaken off the tracks.

The impact was recorded on seismographs throughout the world. In addition a wide range of electrical and magnetic disturbances, as well as unusual twilights and sunsets directly attributable to the blast, was recorded throughout the rest of 1908.

Obviously this was an event of gigantic proportions. Yet one of the most incredible elements of this incredible story is that for years practically no one paid any attention to it. Of course, those people who lived in the immediate vicinity paid attention. But the region was populated mostly by Tunguska tribesmen, a primitive people who lived by reindeer herding.

They were terrified, and immediately began to weave legends around the event. Others in Siberia were also aware that something of major importance had happened. But the blast had taken place some three thousand miles away from Moscow and St. Petersburg, Russia's major population centers. At the best of times communications between Siberia and the cities where the scientists lived and worked were poor, and 1908 was not the best of times for Russia. There had nearly been a revolution in 1905, new forms of government were being tried without much success, and the land was tottering toward the revolution which in 1918 would finally bring down the ancient rule of the Tsars. No one seemed to have the interest or the facilities to investigate an explosion in so obscure a place as Siberia. Throughout the rest of the world scientists simply assumed that there had been an earthquake in Siberia, though they noted with some puzzlement that earthquakes were virtually unknown in that region.

It was nearly twenty years before the outside world again began to hear of the Great Siberian Explosion. The break in the silence was due almost entirely to the obsession of one man, a Soviet scientist named Leonid Kulik. In 1921 Kulik was to lead an expedition to find undiscovered meteorites that had fallen in the Soviet Union. It wasn't going to be a very big expedition. The revolution had left the country economically devastated, without funds for major scientific undertakings. One of the reasons for Kulik's expedition may have been to locate meteorites that could be sold.

A colleague gave Kulik an old calendar in which was reprinted a Siberian newspaper account of the 1908 explosion. The account turned out to be full of errors, but it intrigued the scientist. He believed that he might have a clue to the fall of a large meteorite as yet unknown to science. As Kulik began searching old Siberian newspapers he located a fair number of stories on the 1908 explosion. None of the stories was very complete, but there were enough details for Kulik to recognize that something of considerable, perhaps monumental, importance had happened, and practically no one in the world seemed to know about it.

Kulik was given a small government grant to conduct research into the Siberian explosion. The grant allowed him to get as far as the railway town of Kansk. There he found the event was still remembered vividly. But he also found out that the impact itself had been hundreds of miles to the north. The scientist was now more convinced than ever that he was on the trail of a gigantic meteorite. But he did not have the funds to go any farther. He returned, and then waited for six years before another expedition could be put together.

Kulik's second expedition in 1927 was also piteously underfinanced, but this time he did manage to reach the area where the explosion had taken place. The trip was far harder than even he had imagined. The impact, he was able to determine, had taken place near the Stony Tunguska River, which lay beyond even the most distant trading village. It is an area of taiga, the great pine forest that stretches across much of Siberia. During the winter the deep snow makes the taiga impassable. In the short summer the region turns into one vast mosquito-infested bog —also impassable. Only during the spring, while the ground is still frozen but when there is less chance of violent snowstorms, is traveling through the taiga considered relatively safe. Kulik, an assistant, and a guide set out to find the impact site in March. The trip was painfully slow, only a few miles a day could be covered, but by April 13 he began to see the first signs of the catastrophe.

It was astonishing, beyond his wildest imaginings. For mile after mile the ground was littered with burned and broken trees, all pointing in the same direction, away from the center of the blast. Kulik could see why the Tunguska called the area "the flattened forest."

Trees devastated by the 1908 Siberian explosion (*Sovfoto*).

Kulik pushed farther into the devastated area, expecting that at any time he would come upon a huge crater dug by the meteor he was sure had caused the catastrophe. But he couldn't find the crater because it simply did not exist. The center of the fall was in a vast peat marsh. "The solid ground," he wrote, "heaved outward from the spot in giant waves, like waves of water." There were small holes scattered throughout the area, but no main crater. Kulik theorized that the giant meteorite had broken up somewhere above the surface of the earth, peppering the area with smaller missiles.

Even without a giant meteor crater, what Kulik had found was utterly fantastic. Here were over a hundred square miles devastated by a blast from space. Nearly twenty years after the catastrophe the site of the fall remained one of unparalleled destruction.

By the time Kulik emerged from the taiga his supplies were very nearly exhausted and the rigors of the journey had pushed him to the edge of collapse. Back in Leningrad (what St. Petersburg was renamed after the revolution) his colleagues had begun to wonder whether Leonid Kulik was still alive. When he did return it was in triumph. A once obscure Soviet meteorite expert quite suddenly became a world figure whose words were quoted in papers in London and New York.

And what words they were! They made everyone who heard them shudder. At one lecture he showed motion pictures of the destruction of the forest. Then he said:

"Astronomers and geologists know that this was an exceptional circumstance. But they know also that there is no reason whatever why a similar visitation should not fall at any moment upon a more populous region.

"Thus, had this meteorite fallen in Central Belgium, there would have been no living creature left in the whole country; on London, none left alive in South [of] Manchester or East [of] Bristol. Had it fallen on New York, Philadelphia might have escaped with only its windows shattered, and New Haven and Boston escaped too. But all life in the central area of the meteor's impact would have been blotted out instantaneously."

He wasn't exaggerating either. In our age of thermonuclear weapons we are perhaps a little hardened to hearing about cities blasted out of existence. In 1928 when Kulik gave this lecture people had never heard such talk before from a scientist.

Kulik, however, had never been particularly interested in fame. He was obsessed by the meteorite he was sure had struck Siberia in 1908. Year after year he returned to the site with ever larger and better equipped expeditions. More than once he nearly lost his life, but he never gave up. He made extensive observations and measurements of the flattened forest but he concentrated his efforts on trying to dig into the earth at the center of the area to find the main mass of the meteorite that he was sure was buried there. He never found it. In 1941, during the Nazi invasion of the Soviet Union, Leonid Kulik, serving in the home guards, was wounded in the leg and captured by the Germans. He died on April 24, 1942, in a Nazi prison camp. He was fifty-eight years old.

There is no doubt that Kulik really "discovered" the Great Siberian Explosion, and that without his persistence we would probably know a great deal less about it today than we do. The more years that pass since the time of the event the fainter grows the trail of evidence. Yet his theory as to what caused the catastrophe was almost certainly wrong. Perhaps it was the same stubborn streak which led him to pursue the subject in the first place that made him cling to an untenable theory.

The area of the Siberian explosion has now been thoroughly explored. A road and an airfield have been built to make it more accessible. Today aerial photography can give scientists an overview that was denied to ground-based observers. Men have repeatedly drilled and probed the center of the area without ever finding a single hint that a huge meteoric mass is buried there.

Today the majority of scientists has given up on the theory that the event was caused by the impact of a giant meteorite, or a closely packed mass of meteorites. Even the small craters that so intrigued Kulik are now thought to be natural features of the landscape, and not holes dug by meteorite fragments.

But with the most obvious explanation in disrepute or at least seriously questioned there has been a scramble to provide alternate explanations. The one that has attracted the most scientific backing is that the cause of the explosion was a comet. A meteorite is a solid mass, a comet is not. A comet is a lump of gases frozen solid in the cold of outer space. There may be small solid fragments embedded in the frozen mass, and the structure of a comet has been compared to a dirty snowball. As it approaches the sun some of these gases begin to burn. That is why comets glow and have a "tail."

If a small comet entered the earth's atmosphere, it would almost certainly burn up entirely before reaching the surface of the earth. This would explain why there was no central crater, and no mass of meteoric material. Yet the heat and shock waves created by the comet plunging through the atmosphere would have been great enough to burn and flatten a hundred

A meteor crater in Arizona. No such crater could be found in Siberia (*The American Museum of Natural History*).

square miles of Siberian forest, according to this theory anyway.

If a comet does not excite your imagination, how about a meteorite made of anti-matter? Now anti-matter, in theory, is the exact atomic opposite of the matter from which our own universe is constructed. And, again theoretically, if anti-matter and matter come into contact they will instantly annihilate one another. There has been some experimental work which indicates that anti-matter is more than a theory, but even today that is far from proven. The anti-matter meteor theory of the Siberian explosion was first put forth in the 1940s and attracted a good deal of public attention but only a modest amount of scientific support. Soviet scientists who have spent more time studying the Siberian explosion than anyone else have largely ignored it in favor of comets.

An even more bizarre theory is that the event was caused by the collision with a particle from a "black hole." Black holes are popular at the moment, probably because they are so spectacular and so strange. But a word of caution—black hole theory is at the far frontiers of scientific speculation. It may well turn out to be wrong. But according to theory, a black hole is what results when a gigantic star, one many times the size of our own sun, collapses. Its tremendous gravitational pull causes it to "fall inward" and become an entirely new and unimaginably dense form of matter. A rice-sized speck of this matter might weigh trillions of tons. Inside a black hole none of the laws of physics that we know apply. Said physicist John G. Taylor, "Inside a black hole you have the origin of the universe run backwards."

In 1973 a couple of scientists from the University of Texas suggested the possibility that a tiny fragment of a black hole, perhaps one no larger than an atom, might explain the Siberian blast. What happened to the black hole after it hit the earth? Why, it passed right through like a bullet through butter and came out the other side in the North Atlantic.

But of all the theories to explain the Siberian explosion that have been proposed in recent years, unquestionably the one that has attracted the most attention among the general public anyway is this: The explosion was caused by a nuclear-powered extraterrestrial spaceship that had gone out of control and exploded a few miles above the earth's surface in Siberia. This theory was first proposed by Aleksander Kazantsev, a Soviet science fiction writer. When the theory was first heard of in the West, a lot of people assumed that Kazantsev was a scientist (he was once a mechanic in a metallurgical plant). Westerners did not know that he was writing fiction. Kazantsev, however, may have been serious about the theory he presented as fiction. Actually the theory is not a bad one, and it has been taken up, at least speculatively, by a number of scientists in both the Soviet Union and the West. It was recently made the theme of a popular book entitled *The Fire Came By*. Certainly a spaceship is no more bizarre an answer to the puzzle than an anti-matter meteorite or a piece of a black hole.

John Baxter and Thomas Atkins, authors of *The*

Fire Came By, also theorize that the crew of the doomed spaceship deliberately steered it toward one of the most uninhabited parts of the earth's surface in order to spare us the catastrophe that would result from exploding near a major population center. It's a nice thought, not provable, but nice.

In any event, people are going to be arguing over the cause of the Siberian explosion for a long time to come. Nor are the arguments likely to be resolved either. The earth has never experienced anything remotely like the explosion of 1908. Not in historical times anyway. So we have nothing to compare it with. And considering what happened to one hundred square miles of forest in Siberia, we had all better hope that we never do get anything to compare it with. This is one mystery that can just as well remain unsolved.

2

---◆---

CATTLE MUTILATIONS

In the late summer and early fall of 1974 there was a genuine panic in parts of Nebraska and South Dakota. The reason for the panic was an outbreak of mysterious cattle mutilations. Cattle would be found dead for no obvious reason. Parts of their anatomy were missing.

Both ranchers and local law-enforcement officials were stumped as to the cause of these seemingly bizarre deaths. Soon rumors began to spread that the mutilations were being carried out by members of a Satanist cult which practiced animal sacrifice. A local psychiatrist warned that the mutilations might be the work of a madman, who sooner or later was likely to switch to human victims.

And there were far stranger explanations offered. A few people reported seeing "the Thing," a hairy "man-animal," in the region. Though no one actually said that he saw "the Thing" killing cattle, the connection seemed obvious enough. Bigfoot was roaming the range killing animals.

Then there was the UFO explanation. At about the time the mutilation scare was at its height there were several reports of Unidentified Flying Objects in the region. Somehow the UFOs and the cattle mutilations became connected in the minds of a great many people. They seemed to think that alien creatures from UFOs were killing cattle and then taking off pieces as specimens.

Even in the world of strange beliefs this one seems pretty farfetched. But oddly enough a connection between animal mutilations and UFOs had been made before, several times. Way back in 1897, long before anybody ever heard of UFOs, a number of people throughout the country reported seeing unidentified airships. That was even before the Wright Brothers demonstrated that there could be such things as airships. One of the best-known airship stories from this era was told by a Kansas farmer named Alexander Hamilton. He said that on April 19, 1897, a mysterious airship, "occupied by six of the strangest beings I ever saw," hovered over his cow lot. A rope was dropped from the ship around the neck of a calf in the lot. The struggling calf was lifted off the ground, and both ship and calf disappeared. The next day pieces of the butchered animal were found scattered around a neighboring field.

This astonishing story was told and retold in countless UFO books and lectures. But in the February 1977 issue of *Fate* magazine the old tale was finally revealed as a complete hoax. Hamilton, it seems, was a well-known practical joker and an accomplished liar. He had invented the entire story and got a few of his friends, including the local newspaper editor, to go along with it. People in the area who knew Hamilton's reputation got a good laugh out of the tale but never took it seriously. Everyone was astonished at how much publicity the calf story received.

The subject of mysterious animal mutilations is one of the many that fascinated Charles Fort. He had collected information on the subject all over the world, though most of Fort's cases came from England. In most instances the mutilations were attributed to some sort of unknown animal, often a large black dog. Phantom black dogs are a traditional part of English folklore.

Probably the best known of the English cases took place in 1903 in Wyrley, Staffordshire, England. There a large number of horses, cattle, and sheep were mutilated under mysterious circumstances. A man named George Edalji, the son of an Indian father and English mother, was convicted of the crimes and sent to prison. But there is no doubt that Edalji was an innocent victim of hysteria and racial prejudice. This case attracted the attention of Sir Arthur Conan Doyle, the creator of Sherlock Holmes. Primarily through Conan Doyle's efforts the unfortunate Edalji was ultimately exonerated. This case was never officially solved, though Conan Doyle was quite sure the guilty party was a local man who hated Indians, and that there was nothing unusual or supernatural about what happened.

Fort, however, took a darker view of the animal mutilations. He wrote:

"This is fringing upon an enormous subject that leads away from the slaughtering of sheep to attacks, some of them mischievous, some ordinarily deadly, and some of the Jack the Ripper kind, upon human beings. Though I have hundreds of notes upon mysterious attacks upon human beings, I cannot develop an occult criminology now."

That was typical of Fort, dropping intriguing hints, which ultimately led nowhere at all. Perhaps he wasn't serious. One never could tell. In any case his disciples continued to collect accounts of mysterious mutilations after his death. They were lumped under the heading "phantom butchers." Most of the cases

"Phantom Butchers"

The carcass of an animal is found, sometimes mutilated, sometimes with the allegation made that the blood has been "sucked" out. Sometimes a plausible predator is found on which to blame the incident; most often not. Usually the agent of death disappears without a trace. The phenomenon is nothing new. It probably dates back into immemorial haze. But as we aren't concerned here with establishing historic origins, we will present a run-down beginning with the cases published in Fort's books.

1810. May. Ennerdale, near the border of England and Scotland. Something kills sheep, biting into the jugular vein and sucking blood. 6 or 7 animals per night are involved. A dog is shot. The mortalities cease thereafter. (1)

1874. Jan.-April. Cavan, Ireland. Something was killing up to 30 sheep per night: 42 instances in 3 townships. The animals were described as having their throats "cut," blood "sucked," but no flesh eaten. Dog tracks were found, and a dog was shot, but the killing continued. (1)

1874. April. Near Limerick, more than 100 miles from Cavan, something was reported killing sheep. Several persons claimed to have been bitten by a wolf. They were taken to the Ennis Insane Asylum, "laboring under strange symptoms of insanity." (1)

1904. October. Hexham, Northumberland, England. "...a wolf was ravaging, and [one] was known to have escaped from Shotley Bridge. Something was slaughtering sheep, killing for food, and killing wantonly, sometimes mutilating four or five sheep, and devouring one." (1)

1904. December. As above. Sheep still being killed, despite bloodhounds and the "Hungarian Wolf Hunter." Also at this time, in Wales, occurred a religious revival with attendant hysteria, reports of UFOs, and cases of spontaneous combustion. On both sides of the River Tyne, the same night, sheep were killed. On December 29th, a wolf was found killed on a railroad line. It was a "male gray wolf -- total length five feet -- measurement from foot to top of

shoulder, thirty inches." The sheep depredations ceased -- but the wolf was _not_ the wolf that had escaped earlier.

"There was, in this period, another series of killings. Upon a farm, near Newcastle, late in this year 1904, something was killing poultry." The body of an otter was found on a railroad line. The killings ceased, "coincidence" or not. (1)

1905. March. Kent, England. "Sometimes three or four sheep would be found dying in one flock, having in nearly every case been bitten in the shoulder and disemboweled." (Farm and Home, March 16, 1905.) An Indian jackal was shot, identified as the predator, stuffed, and exhibited. "There is no findable explanation, nor attempted explanation, of how the animal got there." (1)

1903-1907. Wyrley, Staffordshire, England. A famous case of mutilations of horses, cattle, and sheep. One George Edalji was convicted, but later exonerated through publicity emanating from Sir Arthur Conan Doyle. In the summer of 1907, horses were again mutilated and killed. This continued for about a month. (2)

1905. Nov. Badminton, England. Sheep killed. "I have seen two of the carcasses, myself, and can say definitely that it is impossible for it to be the work of a dog. Dogs are not vampires, and do not suck the blood of a sheep, and leave the flesh almost untouched," said Sgt. Carter of the Gloucestershire Police.

The Gloucester Journal said that so many reports had been received that it was hard to believe that only one creature was involved. The editor even reported that "Some even go so far as to call up the traditions of the werewolf, and superstitious people are inclined to this theory."

Another large black dog pops up, being shot on Dec. 16th, but no killings had been reported in the area since Nov. 25th. The killings shifted to Gravesend. By Dec. 16th, 30 sheep had been killed in that vicinity. Nothing was ever found to blame for the carnage. (1)

An *INFO Journal* report on animal mutilations.

remained fairly obscure, attracting only limited local publicity. But there was one which became, at least briefly, a national sensation.

In September of 1967 there was a case in Colorado that closely paralleled the mutilation scare eight years later. A horse named Snippy that had been owned by the Harry King Ranch was missing for several days. The animal's badly mutilated carcass was found on September 9. The cause of death was not immediately apparent and the condition of the horse so bad that members of the King family suspected something unusual and awful had happened to it.

There had been a fair number of UFO sightings in the region just prior to the discovery of Snippy. But most significantly, at that time the University of Colorado was engaged in the first (and to date only) major university study of the UFO phenomenon. So UFOs were very much on the minds of the people of Colorado when Snippy's remains were found.

Several other strangely mutilated horses and cows were also reported in the same area. As the story gathered steam there were more UFO sightings, and the area in which the dead horse was found was rumored to be radioactive. Members of UFO groups descended upon the scene in order to "investigate" and they all issued their own reports. The whole matter became more confused than ever.

Veterinarians came to different conclusions about

what killed Snippy. One suggested that since there had been thunderstorms in the area around the time that the horse died Snippy might have been struck by lightning. The lightning, according to this theory, would have accounted for some of the damage done to the horse. Another vet who examined the carcass of the horse found indications that it had been shot in the back leg. The shooting would not have been the immediate cause of death, but the wound could have become infected and thus led to the animal's death. The veterinarians agreed that many of the "mutilations" had actually been caused by small predatory animals that had attacked the carcass.

Snippy's bones were put on display in a local gift shop, but the excitement surrounding the mysterious death and mutilation soon petered out. When the new mutilation excitement arose nearly a decade later, few recalled the once-famous Snippy the horse.

The mutilation excitement that began in the autumn of 1974 was far more widespread than that generated by Snippy, and it lasted longer. Indeed at the time of this writing the rumors are still flying and there seems no end in sight.

The original Nebraska-South Dakota episode inspired enough fear in the region to require two meetings between veterinarians, local law-enforcement officials, and interested farmers. The reports from two state veterinary laboratories were presented. Both reports stated that every animal brought to the labs had died from natural causes, and that the "mutilations" were made by small predators tearing away the soft parts of the body of the dead animal. Not everyone was convinced by these lab reports, but the majority of local farmers and ranchers seems to have been satisfied and reassured.

During the height of the scare night patrols had been organized throughout the afflicted region in order to catch red-handed the satanic cultists or the alien invaders or whatever at the deadly and dirty business. The patrols never came across anything out of the ordinary.

Finally, the South Dakota Crime Bureau issued a statement which said that in their estimation the cattle deaths were natural, and nothing unusual had in fact happened. The bureau concluded that there was no reason to worry, or to continue investigations any further. After that, local newspapers, which had been having a field day with the story, reported no more mutilations. Whether this was because no one reported mutilations to the papers or because the papers felt that further stories of this type were not newsworthy is unclear. In any case the immediate hysteria died down.

James R. Stewart, an assistant professor of sociology at the University of South Dakota, followed the original outbreak closely. In an article published in the skeptical journal *The Zetetic*, Stewart concluded that the entire episode was a "collective delusion." How had it begun?

"There are two possible answers to this question. First, perhaps given the conditions of strain and anxiety, farmers with firsthand experience and knowledge were simply caught up in the delusionary spiral. Second, there exists the possibility that some farmers reported mutilations because their insurance policies would reimburse them for acts of vandalism but not for deaths resulting from natural causes. I have no evidence that claims were paid for mutilations, but this possibility might motivate some to report mutilated, and not simply dead, cattle.

"Other mundane explanations include the possibility that in one or two instances the cattle were actually killed by people or even a pack of wild dogs. Not infrequently cattle are slaughtered in the field by persons who are stealing beef because of the high prices. This explanation is even more likely when one considers that the over-the-counter meat prices reached unprecedented highs during the period of the mutilations. There have also been isolated reports at various times of packs of dogs running wild, and it's conceivable that they might possibly have been responsible for a small number of the deaths."

But such mundane explanations have not satisfied a large number of people, most of them far removed from cattle-raising areas. Interest in Satanism has declined recently, so the blood cult explanation is not heard as frequently. But interest in UFOs is again on the rise. So the mutilations are now most often linked to UFOs, usually on the flimsiest of evidence.

Dead and partially eaten cattle are an everyday feature of ranch life. Just why people suddenly begin to offer bizarre explanations for this everyday occurrence is impossible to determine. But once the story starts it rapidly develops into a mild mass hysteria. There are a lot of people who feel genuinely uneasy about the world. Anything odd is likely to look to them like part of a plot by Satanists, aliens from another world, or whatever. Besides, such explanations are more exciting. Others, particularly those who work for sensationalist publications, are less interested in pursuing the truth than they are in creating an exciting story. They pump up the mystery by the addition, or more often the subtraction, of important details.

This particular little hysteria is having a pretty good run. When it finally dies out, as other mutilation scares have in the past, it will not die forever. It is safe to predict that the cattle mutilation mystery will be back again to puzzle and tantalize a new generation of mystery lovers.

3

---·◆·---

FROZEN MAMMOTHS

I see a lot of horror movies. It is a not-so-secret vice of mine. I have seen, oh, I don't know how many that have a scene something like this:

The scientific expedition is slogging wearily through the snows of the Arctic (or the Antarctic). While passing a sheer ice wall the scientists spy what looks like the form of some unknown creature frozen within. They cut the thing out in a huge block of ice and ship it back to the laboratory in New York in a refrigerated steamer. Then there is an unexpected power failure in the laboratory. The ice thaws, the creature that has been frozen for millennia awakes, and a new horror is unleashed upon the world. In the last scene the prehistoric creature is destroyed through the use of tactical nuclear weapons.

Even if you are not a horror movie fan you have probably seen some variation on that theme yourself. The idea that creatures frozen for centuries can be brought back to life by thawing (or any other method for that matter) is, scientifically speaking, nonsense. But that creatures extinct for thousands of years have been found frozen in northern regions is a well-established fact. These creatures are usually woolly mammoths, well-furred relatives of the modern elephant. A smaller number of woolly rhinoceroses have also been found, but it is the mammoths that have always captured the most attention. A few years ago there was a good deal of excitement over the claim that a frozen Abominable Snowman had been found. That story, however, turned out to be a hoax. The frozen mammoths are no hoax. They have been reported since 1692.

Not so very long ago, geologically speaking, that is, woolly mammoths ranged widely over northern regions. During the Ice Age they were quite common in North America. Then about ten thousand years ago they all died out. So did the woolly rhinoceroses and a lot of other large animals. Just why they died out is unknown. It wasn't just because the ice melted and the climate got warmer—there are still plenty of cold regions on earth. There is no obvious reason why the mammoths could not have continued to live

The woolly mammoth and cave drawings of mammoths (*Drawing by James G. Teason, from* THE AGE OF GIANT MAMMALS).

on, though in a more restricted range. But that's another problem. Our task here is to explore the subject of frozen mammoths and how they got that way.

The controversy over this subject is a surprisingly emotional one. On the surface it might not seem that frozen mammoths are the sort of objects that would generate much passion, but they do because the subject touches directly on an argument that has been going on for a long time between the catastrophists and the uniformitarians.

At one time it had simply been assumed that the earth was periodically swept by global catastrophes, like the flood described in the Bible. According to this theory the catastrophes had shaped many of the earth's features and had caused the extinction of many forms of life, among them the woolly mammoth.

But about two hundred years ago scientists began to abandon catastrophism. They realized that the earth was far, far older than had originally been suspected and came to the conclusion that most of the earth's features were formed slowly over great periods of time rather than almost instantly as a result of global catastrophes. The geologists were first to come to this conclusion, but after Charles Darwin and his evolutionary theory took hold, the biologists decided that both evolution and extinction were also slow gradual processes.

Today there has been a very modest retreat from the strict uniformitarian view, and many scientists actively entertain the possibility of at least limited catastrophic changes, particularly as far as the extinction of large numbers of species is concerned. In general, however, most scientists still hold to the basic tenets of uniformitarianism.

But radical catastrophism is far from dead. Most of those who label themselves Forteans, and others who dabble in unorthodox scientific speculation, are dyed-in-the-wool catastrophists. They defend their position with great vigor and cite the frozen mammoths as one of the most dramatic pieces of evidence in support of their theories.

These great beasts, they say, were literally frozen in their tracks by a sudden and catastrophic change in climate. (Never mind what caused the change—many theories have been offered—the main point here is that they say it was a sudden and dramatic change.) The animals have been found frozen intact, often with the meal they were last eating still between their teeth. The meal, in this view, consisted of plants that could not possibly grow in cold climates, another indication of a sudden climate change. The mammoths were frozen so quickly that their flesh remained fresh, and has occasionally been eaten by those who found them. The late Ivan Sanderson, one of the more prolific and colorful of the Forteans, wrote

Mammoth bones from Siberia.

"worst of all, many of these animals were perfectly fresh, whole and undamaged, and still either standing or at least kneeling upright."

No one has yet claimed that one of these creatures has been thawed out and taken to the zoo, but the claims are very nearly as sensational, and it might be useful to take a closer look at them.

The bones and tusks of thousands of mammoths have been recovered from the frozen ground of northern areas. In fact, there was once a brisk trade in mammoth ivory from Siberia. But bones and tusks are

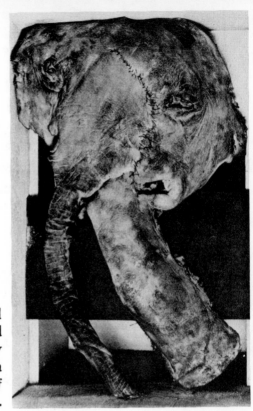

The partially reconstructed remains of a well-preserved frozen baby woolly mammoth found in Alaska (*The American Museum of Natural History*).

one thing, frozen carcasses are quite another. A report that appeared in a 1961 issue of *Science*, the official publication of the American Association for the Advancement of Science, lists only thirty-nine discoveries of mammoth remains in which some of the soft parts of the creature were preserved by freezing. There have been a few more discoveries since that time, but nothing spectacular. So instead of thousands of frozen mammoths, the number of frozen mammoths of any kind actually discovered is well under fifty. Most of these came from Siberia, with a smaller number from Alaska.

Of these remains only five can be considered to be reasonably complete. Of these five, one, the mammoth recovered from the Berezovka River in 1806, is far and away the most complete and the best known. Whenever you read a sensational description of a frozen woolly mammoth the odds are ten to one that it is the Berezovka mammoth that is being described.

Unfortunately for the catastrophists, the Berezovka mammoth quite clearly did not freeze to death. The bones of its legs were broken, and it showed definite signs of having died of asphyxiation. The evidence indicates that the creature fell off a cliff, severely injuring itself, and was within a short period of time buried, probably in a mud slide.

But if there was no massive climate change how was the creature quick-frozen? Under normal conditions the carcass would have rotted away thousands of years ago. Here, too, we must examine the evidence a bit more closely. The freshness of the frozen mammoths has been much exaggerated. There are stories that explorers ate steaks cut from the carcass of the frozen giant. This is a pure invention. Many firsthand reports say that the meat of the mammoth looked fresh enough, but the stench it gave off when thawed was unbearable. None of the men would

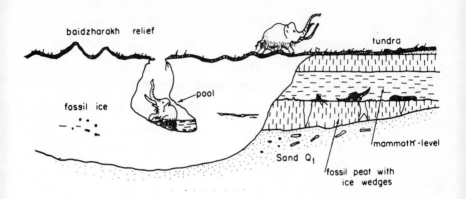

Diagram showing one method by which mammoths could have been killed and preserved. The "baidzharakh" terrain contains layers of ice. The ice is eroded by streams. The beds of the streams can become covered with a thin layer of ice through which a heavy animal like a mammoth might fall (*From* PLEISTOCENE EXTINCTIONS).

touch the meat, though the sled dogs ate what was given to them. Chemical examination of some of the tissue from the mammoth showed "deep penetrating chemical alteration as a result of the very slow decay." In other specimens the decay was far more advanced than it was on the Berezovka mammoth. So the mammoths were not quick-frozen at all.

Still, the fact that we possess the frozen remains, no matter what shape they are in, of animals that died thousands of years ago is quite extraordinary. How did it come about?

Scientists have offered a number of theories, none of them complete, but a general consensus would go something like this: Most of the mammoths whose remains have been frozen died by falling over cliffs into crevasses or drowning in bogs and rivers. The only frozen animals found were mammoths and a smaller number of woolly rhinoceroses. There were plenty of other animals living in the same area at the time—horses, antelopes, several variety of deer, and so on. Their bones are numerous. Yet it is only the heavy, stiff-legged "giants" that have been preserved. This hints that there must have been something about their structure that made them more likely to freeze. Scientists believe that the large, heavy, and probably clumsy animals would be most likely to fall into holes, and the least likely to be able to get out. The contents of the frozen animals' stomachs indicate that most of them died in the late summer or early fall, just when temperatures are at their highest and the footing in northern regions at its most treacherous.

Once the creature had fallen into a hole and died there, its carcass would be covered by mud which would tend to protect the remains from rapid decay. As colder weather came on the mud would freeze around the remains. In polar regions there is the permafrost, a level below which the ground never thaws. If conditions were right, the mammoth remains would be encased in the permafrost, and thus preserved indefinitely. Thousands of years later, thaws or slides would expose the remains to the amazement of people who had never seen a living mammoth.

When frozen mammoth remains were first discovered they inspired a host of myths. Some people believed that the mammoths were not ancient animals but huge creatures that lived underground like moles, and had frozen to death only when they blundered to the surface. Once the remains were firmly identified as those of the long extinct woolly mammoth, the underground giant myth died out. The myth that the mammoths were frozen to death in some kind of catastrophic weather change has been harder to kill. Indeed many people today still hold to it. But it's hard to support in view of evidence.

William R. Farrand, writing in *Science,* sums up the case for the orthodox in these words:

"The well-preserved specimens, with food in their stomachs and between their teeth, must have died suddenly probably from asphyxia resulting from drowning in a lake or bog or from being buried alive by a mudflow or cave-in of a river bank. Since only the heavy-footed giants of the fauna—the mammoths and woolly rhinoceroses—have been found in a frozen state, it is very unlikely that a catastrophic coagulation occurred in Siberia. On the contrary, the frozen giants are indicative of a normal and expected (uniformitarian) circumstance of life on the tundra."

4

ELEPHANTS IN AMERICA

Personally I have never considered elephants to be the least bit mysterious. They are the most comfortably down-to-earth creatures I can imagine, with the possible exception of hedgehogs. Yet we have just gotten through with one elephant mystery, and here is another.

It has long been established that man and mammoth were contemporaries in Europe. The woolly mammoth as well as several other now extinct creatures are prominent subjects in cave art. But were man and elephant ever contemporary in America? Yes, I know that mammoths and mastodons are not, strictly speaking, elephants. But they are close relatives of the modern elephant and they look more like elephants than anything else alive. I use the word elephant for convenience.

The subject of elephants in America has been debated for a long time. At first the conclusions people arrived at were determined more by their underlying philosophical assumptions than by the evidence. This is probably because there wasn't much evidence one way or the other. Thomas Jefferson, who had one of the best scientific minds in the America of his day, had often examined the bones of elephants found in his native Virginia. He was convinced that the huge animals could still be found alive and roaming about the then unexplored territory to the west.

Jefferson believed this because he did not believe in the extinction of species. He thought that nature was too perfect to allow for such a wasteful process as extinction. Of course Jefferson was dead wrong.

When the fact that species do indeed become extinct became established, most scientists assumed that man and elephant had never been contemporaries in America. The underlying reasoning was that man had not been in the Americas for very long, and therefore all ancient elephant-like creatures must have died out long before man arrived.

But that assumption, too, proved to be incorrect. Within the last fifty years unmistakable evidence has been found that man and elephant were not only contemporaries, but that elephants were widely hunted. Right now the most popular theory to account for the extinction of the elephants and other large mammals in the Americas holds that they were wiped out by human hunters.

Then where is the controversy? The controversy centers over when the elephants died out. The conventional scientific belief is that all of the elephants were dead and gone about ten thousand years ago, and that they were not only gone, but entirely forgotten by the American Indians long before Europeans arrived.

The unconventional belief is that the elephants hung on lots longer, that they were well known at least to the immediate ancestors of the Indians who lived at the time of Columbus, and that elephants were frequently represented in Indian art. A smaller number hold that elephants of one sort or another were still alive in America when the Europeans came. A tiny minority of radical Forteans contend that some woolly mammoths might still be alive today, though in Siberia, not Alaska.

A century ago the controversy over elephants in the Americas had a different character than it does today, and it was much more emotional. Then it was mainly an argument over the diffusionist theory of culture. Diffusionists hold that culture developed in one place and then spread throughout the world by migration. For that reason the cultures of the American Indians are directly and intimately linked to the cultures of the Old World. The opposing point of view holds that while migration may have played some part in the development of human culture, most can be attributed to separate development. For example, diffusionists say that the pyramids of South America are direct copies of the pyramids of Egypt or vice versa. Their opponents say that the structures have only superficial similarities, and are the result of separate development.

Diffusionism was, and is, a perfectly respectable scientific point of view. There collected under its banner, however, a large number of theorists who were not at all respectable. Included in this group was Ignatius Donnelly, the world's number-one partisan of the lost continent of Atlantis.

According to Donnelly, civilization really originated in Atlantis. After that unfortunate continent sank, refugees from the disaster spread their civilization all over the world. Elephants were very important to Donnelly's theory. In his book on Atlantis first published in 1882 he wrote:

"We find in America numerous representations of the elephant. We are forced to one of two conclusions: Either the monuments date back to the time of the mammoth in North America, or these people did intercourse at some time in the past with races who

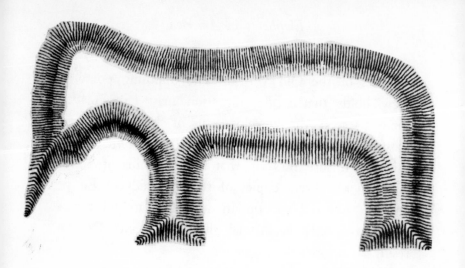

Drawing of the Wisconsin elephant mound.

possessed the elephant, and from whom they obtained pictures of that singular animal. Plato tells us that Atlanteans possessed great numbers of elephants.

"There are in Wisconsin a number of mounds of earth representing different animals—men, birds, and quadrupeds. Among the latter is a mound representing an elephant, 'so perfect in its proportions, and complete in its representation of an elephant, that its builders must have been well acquainted with all the physical characteristics of the animal which they delineated.'

"On a farm in Louisa County, Iowa, a pipe was plowed up which represents an elephant. It was found in a section where the ancient mounds were very abundant and rich in relics. The pipe is of sand-

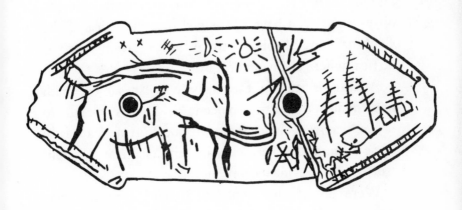

The Lenape stone from Bucks County, Pennsylvania, presumably showing men and elephants.

stone, of the ordinary Mound Builder's type, and has every appearance of age and usage. There can be no doubt of its genuineness."

Donnelly would have added information about carvings of elephants made by the Mayans of Central America, had the discoveries been made before he wrote his book. Other supporters of Atlantis have made much of these, however.

Now I don't happen to believe in the lost continent of Atlantis. I certainly don't believe in Atlantis being the homeland of all civilization, but I'm not going to argue that point here. The fact that it has now been established beyond a reasonable doubt that man and elephant were contemporaries in the Americas takes a lot of the force out of Donnelly's argument. Indeed, it weakens the argument of other diffusionists who have contended that the "idea of the elephant" was brought to America from Asia or Africa, where elephants still exist.

Atlantis is still an extremely popular subject with unorthodox theorists. Someone is always trying to prove that the civilizations of South America really came from somewhere else, but the elephant is rarely trotted out as evidence any more.

Were all of the elephant drawings and artifacts mentioned by Donnelly and others therefore Indian representations of the mammoth and the mastodon that once were native to the Americas rather than the contemporary elephant that is native only to Asia and Africa? Most scientists would say very firmly that they are not. Where then do all these elephant representations originate? They originate, say the scientists, in the eye of the beholder or the hand of the hoaxer, and there are no authentic representations of elephants to be found anywhere in pre-Columbian America.

For a while the best known of the "American elephants" were found in carvings at the celebrated Mayan city of Tikal. Carved in relief on a large slab of stone is what appears, at first glance, to be the representation of a pair of elephant heads. Each elephant is topped by a Mayan mahout riding on the beast's neck. If one is looking for elephants in Mayan art, the Tikal carvings can seem quite impressive. But if you look a little closer there are some oddities about these Tikal elephants. For example, they have nostrils at the base of their "trunks," rather than at the tip, where they should be. They also appear to have feathers. If you are not looking for elephants, you might come to the conclusion that these carvings represent highly stylized macaws, large parrot-like birds that were common in Central America and were often represented in Mayan art.

Many of the other Mayan "elephants" can be similarly disposed of. Mayan art is strange to those brought up in a European artistic tradition. Most of it

The Mayan carving at Tikal showing what may be elephants or may be macaws. Note nostril at top of "trunk" and large round eyes surrounded by feathers (*From* ANCIENT RUINS AND ARCHAEOLOGY).

Two drawings of the same Mayan glyph. One looks like an elephant, the second, more accurate, one does not (*From* ANCIENT RUINS AND ARCHAEOLOGY).

is also poorly preserved. When the carvings were first discovered they were usually copied by artists, often under very difficult conditions. Therefore the copies are not very accurate. These poor copies were all that most people ever got to see. What looked like elephants could be found in these copies. Some of the drawings were also made by people already obsessed with diffusionist ideas. They were convinced that they were seeing elephants because they knew elephants *should* be there. But these early conclusions have not stood up upon re-examination.

Critics contend that the "elephant mound" mentioned by Donnelly and others is in reality a bear mound to which flooding or some other accident of nature has added a trunk-like extension at the front end. Bears were common subjects for Indian mounds.

The "elephant pipes" found in Iowa are both harder and easier to dispose of. Harder because they unquestionably show elephants, easier because they are probably fakes. The pipes were found in Indian mounds in 1878 and 1880. At that time many people thought that the mounds had been built by some great vanished civilization from somewhere else. We now know, beyond any reasonable doubt, that the mounds were built by the ancestors of the Indians who lived in the area.

The man who discovered the elephant pipes was the Reverend Jacob Gass, a zealous supporter of the vanished civilization theory. The Reverend Mr. Gass had done a good deal of digging in mounds around Davenport, Iowa, and he always seemed to come up with things that no one else was able to find. In addition to his elephant pipes he found inscribed tablets containing Roman, Arabic, Phoenician, and Hebrew characters. Even at the time, scientists came very close to accusing the Reverend Mr. Gass of deliberate fraud.

The mound-building Indians buried artifacts made from many different kinds of animals in their mounds. The mounds have been extensively excavated, but not a single scrap of ivory or identifiable remains of any member of the elephant clan has ever been found. This is a strong indication that by the time the mounds were built the mammoths and mastodons that once roamed North America were either very rare or, more likely, entirely extinct.

There are a number of other drawings and artifacts presumably showing men and elephants that have turned up around the Americas. There are even some "Indian drawings" that are supposed to show men fighting dinosaurs! But scientists have given such items even less credence than the Reverend Gass's elephant pipes.

So, while the claim that elephants have been depicted on a variety of pre-Columbian items has often been put forth, it is, to say the very least, highly questionable.

Leaving the realm of artifacts we venture into the even murkier realm of myths, legends, and travelers' tales. The Indians of Canada apparently had tales of something they called the Big Elk. This huge beast was supposed to be very dangerous, could navigate through eight feet of snow, had a very tough skin, which weapons could hardly penetrate, and "has some sort of arm which comes out of his shoulder and which he uses as we do."

The Delaware Indians had legends concerning a herd of huge shaggy animals that were so powerful they drove off all the other animals in the vicinity. Finally the god of the Indians became so incensed that he killed off most of the creatures, and after a tremendous struggle managed to wound the leader of the herd, which fled.

There are many problems in using Indian legends (or any other kind of legend) as evidence for anything. Perhaps the greatest problem in this case is that the people who collected them and wrote them down were often not very knowledgeable, and not very careful.

Then there is the story attributed to an English sailor named Ingram, who in 1580 was supposed to have walked from the Gulf of Mexico to Nova Scotia. Along the way he reported seeing huge shaggy animals with large floppy ears being hunted by the Indians in what is now Pennsylvania. There are even more intriguing tales of Siberian hunters and travelers coming across living woolly mammoths within the last few hundred years. A nineteenth-century story of the killing of a woolly mammoth in Alaska was, however, a complete fabrication, though it was widely believed. People kept asking the Smithsonian Institution, where the creature was supposed to have been sent, to put it on display. When Smithsonian officials replied that they didn't have any fresh woolly mammoth, the questioners often got angry and insisted that they were being confronted with a cover-up.

So, while there are a lot of bits and pieces hinting that mammoths or mastodons may have survived well beyond the date usually given for their extinction, none of these bits and pieces is conclusive. Taken all together they still make up only a very weak case. But it would be foolish to be dogmatic on this point. After all, at one time it seemed inconceivable that man and elephant could ever have been contemporaries in the Americas. We don't really know why the mammoths and mastodons became extinct in the first place, and therefore it is possible that isolated pockets of them survived far beyond the usual ten-thousand-year date given for their death.

5

---·◆·---

THE DOPPELGANGER

Once, while walking down Fifty-seventh Street in Manhattan, I had an eerie experience. I saw, coming directly toward me, someone who looked very familiar, but I couldn't quite place the face. I'm usually very good at recognizing people, so this lapse bothered me. As I drew closer I saw by his expression that the fellow was as puzzled as I. It was all very frustrating and disturbing, because there was no doubt in my mind that I knew the person.

Then, quite suddenly, I realized who it was that was coming toward me—it was me! I was looking at my own reflection in a plate-glass window. I felt foolish, of course, but the incident also gave me a very creepy feeling. Since then I have often thought that suddenly meeting your own double could be one of the most unsettling experiences that life holds. The idea has always fascinated and rather frightened me. I remember that as a child I had heard, I have no idea where or from whom, that everybody has a perfect double somewhere in the world. I think I believed that for a long time.

There was nothing supernatural or even unusual about my "meeting" on Fifty-seventh Street. But there have been a surprisingly large number of cases in which people have reported meeting, not their reflection, but their exact double.

Probably the most celebrated story of this type concerns the French writer Guy de Maupassant. In 1885 De Maupassant was working on his masterful horror story "The Horla." Quite unexpectedly a figure opened the door to his study, walked across the room, and sat down in front of him. The figure then began dictating the words of the story to De Maupassant.

The writer was astounded. How could this person have gotten into his study? How could he know the very words De Maupassant intended to write? Who was he? It was then that he realized the stranger sitting across from him was no stranger at all but his exact double. The whole scene disappeared quickly, but it left De Maupassant a thoroughly shaken man.

There is a rational explanation for this experience. De Maupassant was in the early stages of a disease that was eventually to lead to his insanity and death.

Even at this point the disease might have been responsible for hallucinations. That is how most of De Maupassant's biographers have interpreted the story.

Yet the belief that we can and do sometimes meet our double is an extremely ancient and widespread one. It appears to exist among many primitive peoples. The first recorded case that we know of comes down from Aristotle. He tells the tale of a man who felt that he could not go outside without meeting himself.

The belief in a personal double was particularly well developed in German folklore, where the phenomenon was given the name *doppelganger*, a name that has stuck. In German folk belief the doppelganger was usually a warning of impending death. John Godwin, a collector of odd tales, has this to say about the doppelganger. "In the original version the doppelganger is a spectral figure, seemingly solid and quite unlike a ghost, but without vivid coloration. He resembles a slightly faded photograph of the original. Sometimes he appears to give warning of impending danger. More often he materializes as a challenger, a symbol of the conflict between two beings sharing one soul. In macabre legend the two meet in some lonely spot, they quarrel, and the human kills his double—and in doing so kills himself."

Not only was the subject a common feature of

Germanic folklore; it was also taken up by a large number of writers, Dostoievsky, Kafka, Oscar Wilde, Edgar Allan Poe, and many writers of lesser stature. Psycholgist Graham Reed speculates that the reason the subject of the doppelganger exercised such a morbid fascination on such a large number of writers was that many of them actually had the experience of seeing their own doubles.

To the story of De Maupassant, Reed adds the experience of the great German poet Goethe, who met himself on the road while riding a horse. Goethe has always been considered a man of unusual mental stability. The English poet Percy Bysshe Shelley was a more dramatic figure and he had a more dramatic and alarming encounter. He was visiting the Italian city of Pisa when he was approached by a figure wearing a long cloak and hood which concealed his face. When the figure was within a few feet of the poet it raised its hood, revealing Shelley's own face. *"Siete sodisfatto?"* asked the double, "Are you satisfied?"

Despite the fact that there is considerable evidence that the doppelganger experience is a fairly common one, most scientists regarded it as little more than a piece of gloomy folklore until the end of the last century. Even now it has been studied only by a small number of European psychologists. The phenomenon has been almost completely ignored by British or American authorities.

"Not to Be Reproduced," a painting by the Belgian surrealist René Magritte (*The Edward James Foundation*).

From these European studies Reed draws a picture of the doppelganger.

"Usually the doppelganger apparition appears without warning and takes the form of a mirror-image of the viewer, facing him and just beyond arm's reach. It is life-sized, but very often only the face or the head and trunk are 'seen.' Details are very clear, but the colors are either dull or absent. Generally the image is transparent; some people have described it as being 'jelly-like' or as though projected onto glass. In most cases the double imitates the subject's movements and facial expressions in mirror imagery, as though it were his reflection in a glass."

Some of those who have reported seeing their doubles also say that they can hear or actually touch them. Most are immediately convinced that the figures they see are themselves.

Doppelganger experiences are fairly common among people with certain neurological conditions—epilepsy, for example. Julius Caesar, who was an epileptic, was reported to have seen his own double pacing up and down in front of him before the onset of a seizure. This gave him time to prepare himself for the attack.

Normal people have also reported doppelganger experiences, though less frequently. Usually these experiences have occurred late at night or early in the morning, and during periods of fatigue or great stress.

As in the old folk tales of the doppelganger, the experience is almost always a gloomy and depressing one.

The ancients, of course, regarded the doppelganger as some sort of spirit or supernatural projection of an individual. Modern psychologists feel that, while they cannot explain the doppelganger effect, it is an unusual, but not at all supernatural, experience.

But not everyone is convinced of the psychological explanation. John Godwin cites a couple of modern doppelganger accounts which have the old air of supernatural mystery about them. The first concerns Catherine Reinhardt, a California artist who says she has had such experiences repeatedly. But her experiences had a very curious twist. Each time she saw her double it looked about five years older than she did at that moment.

The most striking experience came when she was twenty-eight. She saw her double at a cocktail party. The double looked a little older and walked with a slight limp. Four years later Catherine Reinhardt was in a serious auto accident. Her husband was killed and her leg badly injured. She never fully recovered from the injury and continued to walk with a slight limp, just as her double had done.

Godwin's second tale he obtained from a man named Alex B. Griffith. In this case the doppelganger, instead of being an omen of disaster, turned out to deliver a timely warning—twice.

In the summer of 1944 Griffith was an infantry sergeant leading a patrol in France. Though the countryside through which Griffith and his men were passing was known to be infested with the enemy there was no sign of danger, and everyone felt quite relaxed.

Quite unexpectedly, Griffith saw a figure on the road ahead of him. The figure was waving its arms and shouting. Though no words could be heard, the figure was obviously trying to make Griffith and his men stop and go back. The figure was, of course, the perfect image of Griffith, right down to the small bandage that he had on his chin at that moment. No one else in the patrol had seen the figure, and therefore the men were quite surprised when their sergeant ordered them to go back. Griffith himself could not explain why he had so immediately responded to the figure's warning. He only knew that if he went forward, he and all his men would be killed.

As he sat on the ground trying to figure out what to do next, an American supply vehicle passed the stopped foot soldiers and headed down the road to the spot where the doppelganger had given its warning. There was a sudden burst of machine-gun fire and the jeep spun wildly out of control, its driver

"How They Met
Themselves," by the
English painter Dante
Gabriel Rossetti (*The
Fitzwilliam Museum*).

killed in the blast. Somewhere up ahead a German machine gun was hidden to guard the road, and if Griffith and his men had gone any farther they would have been gunned down.

Twenty years later Griffith and his family were on a camping trip in Canada. They had begun their trip at the end of a tremendous storm, and as they hiked single file through the woods the winds were still very gusty.

The trail led them to a clearing, and in it Griffith, who was leading, saw himself again. It was not Griffith as he was then, but Sergeant Griffith, as he had been in France twenty years earlier, complete with combat gear and bandaged chin. As before, the figure was waving its arms and shouting "Back! Back!" soundlessly. No one else saw the figure. Once again Griffith reacted instinctively to comply with the figure's warning.

A few seconds later, a huge tree weakened by the storm came crashing down into the clearing where Griffith and his family would have been if they had not been stopped.

Now it is quite easy to find natural explanations for both of these accounts: exaggeration, selective memory, the possibility that Griffith had been subconsciously aware of certain signs of danger but his mind had made these fears conscious in the form of an hallucination. No one could possibly build a case for a supernatural doppelganger upon such evidence.

Yet these tales, and others like them, hold a creepy fascination for me, and from the eternal popularity of the doppelganger theme, it is obvious that they have fascinated many others as well.

6

HUMAN
SPONTANEOUS COMBUSTION

"They advance slowly, looking at all these things. The cat remains where they found her, still snarling at the something on the ground, before the fire and between the two chairs. What is it? Hold up the light.

"Here is a small burnt patch of flooring; here is the tinder from a little bundle of burnt paper, but not so light as usual, seeming to be steeped in something; and here is—is it the cinder of a small charred and broken log of wood sprinkled with white ashes, or is it coal? O Horror, he is here! and this, from which we run away, striking out the light and over-turning one another into the street, is all that repre-sents him.

"Help, help, help! come into this house for Heaven's sake!

"Plenty will come in, but none can help. The Lord Chancellor of that court, true to his title in his last act, has died the death of all Lord Chancellors in all courts and of all authorities in all places under all names soever, where false pretenses are made, and where injustice is done. Call the day by any name Your Highness will, attribute it to whom you will, or say it might have been prevented how you will, it is the same death eternally—inborn, inbred, engendered in the corrupted humours of the vicious body itself, and that only—Spontaneous Combustion, and none other of all the deaths that can be died."

So Charles Dickens described finding the remains, or rather what very little remained, of the rag-and-bone man Mr. Krook, in his novel *Bleak House*. Mr. Krook's demise had been brought about by what Dickens called spontaneous combustion. According to Dickens the chemicals of Mr. Krook's body had combined in such a way as to cause him to burn up immediately and completely without any outside intervention at all.

This wasn't just a fantastic literary device cooked up by Dickens in order to get rid of a character in an appropriately dramatic fashion. Dickens believed that this form of death was not only possible but that it had happened many times. As every science student knows, spontaneous combustion does take place in na-

Mr. Krook's flaming end. A drawing for Charles Dickens'
novel *Bleak House* (*New York Public Library*).

ture. But does it take place in living things? That is the question. Dickens realized that many of his contemporaries, particularly the scientifically minded, did not believe in human spontaneous combustion, so a little later in *Bleak House* he went on to defend the proposition. Describing an inquest into Krook's death:

"Some of these authorities (of course the wisest) hold with indignation that the deceased had no business to die in the alleged manner; and being reminded by other authorities of a certain inquiry into the evidence for such deaths, reprinted in the sixth volume of the *Philosophical Transactions;* and also of a book not quite unknown, on *English Medical Jurisprudence;* and likewise of the Italian case of the Countess Cornelia Baudi as set forth in detail by one Bianchini . . ." and so on at considerable length.

Dickens was quite correct in anticipating that using death by human spontaneous combustion would be controversial. When *Bleak House* came out he was widely attacked and ridiculed for getting rid of his character in such a manner. Dickens was genuinely stung by the criticism, but instead of simply letting the matter drop he answered back repeatedly. In the preface to a second edition of *Bleak House* he wrote:

"I have no need to observe that I do not wilfully or negligently mislead my readers, and that, before I wrote that description, I took pains to investigate the subject. There are about thirty cases on record, of which the most famous, that of the Countess Cornelia de Baudi Cesenate, was minutely investigated and described by Giuseppe Bianchini, a prebendary of Verona, otherwise distinguished in letters, who published an account of it at Verona, in 1731, which he afterwards republished at Rome. The appearances, beyond all rational doubt, observed in that case, are the appearances observed in Mr. Krook's case. The next most famous instance happened at Rheims six years earlier; and the historian in that case is Le Cat, one of the most renowned surgeons produced by France. The subject was a woman whose husband was ignorantly convicted of having murdered her; but, on solemn appeal to a higher court, he was acquitted, because it was shown upon the evidence that she had died the death to which this name of Spontaneous Combustion is given. . . . I shall not abandon the facts until there shall have been a considerable Spontaneous Combustion of the testimony on which human occurrences are usually received."

Dickens also found a case nearer his own time which had taken place in Columbus, Ohio. "The subject was a German, who kept a liquorshop and was an inveterate drunkard."

Despite the virtually unanimous opinion of the scientific community that human spontaneous combustion didn't happen, and couldn't happen, Dickens simply refused to let go. The more he was attacked the more tightly he clung to the idea. Critics were puzzled and amused by his persistence. It was frequently commented upon in the press, which took a livelier interest in the opinions of authors than the press generally does today.

But Dickens was far from the only one fascinated by the idea of human spontaneous combustion. It was one of those subjects that held a deep attraction for Victorian Englishmen. The sensational newspapers of the day often carried accounts of people who had suddenly gone up in flames, in much the same way as the sensational newspapers of today often carry accounts of people who have been kidnapped by UFOs or ships that have disappeared into the Bermuda Triangle. The quality of evidence in these accounts was about the same, that is to say, not very good at all.

The idea of human spontaneous combustion arose, at least in part, from the old and erroneous notion that all life processes were controlled by four basic body substances or humors. When these humors were out of balance the results could be disease and presumably a fiery end as well. The thought that vicious people could literally burn up as a consequence of their own unbalanced body chemistry appealed to the Victorian's moral sense.

The theory of the humors had begun with the ancient Greeks, but should have been pretty well discredited by Dickens' time and absolutely archaic in our own. Yet the belief in human spontaneous combustion persists as a subterranean belief even today.

I don't remember when I first heard it, but it was surely when I was very young, because by the time I was ten or eleven I had begun to worry about it. I somehow got the notion that if you wore too many heavy clothes in the house you might burn up—quite literally. Since my mother seemed convinced that the slightest chill would be fatal, I had to dress pretty warmly in winter. I had also picked up the idea (heaven knows from where) that if you wore rubber galoshes in the house for too long you would go blind. Every winter I would spend an awful lot of time taking off coats, sweaters, and galoshes, convinced that if I didn't I would either catch fire or go blind.

Gullible children are not the only ones who have taken human spontaneous combustion seriously. So have some collectors of odd phenomena. A 1966 case was reported by Larry E. Arnold in the Fortean journal *Pursuit*. The same case was later reprinted in *Fate* magazine, the nation's number-one popular source of articles on the weird. The place was Coudersport, Pennsylvania, and the person involved, ninety-two-year-old Dr. J. Irving Bentley. What little remained of Dr. Bentley was discovered by Don E. Gosnell, a gas company meter reader, in a scene very reminiscent of the discovery of Mr. Krook, described by Dickens. Part of Dr. Bentley's leg remained unburned, but that was about all. A hole had been burned right through the floor, and most of Dr. Bentley's ashes had fallen into the basement. The rest of the room was untouched by flame.

The local coroner described the remains: "All I found was a knee joint, which was atop a post in the basement, the lower leg with its foot on the bathroom floor, and the now-scattered ashes six feet below."

The conventional explanation for Dr. Bentley's death was that the ninety-two-year-old man, a semi-invalid who lived alone, had accidentally set fire to his clothes. He was a regular pipe smoker. He tried to extinguish the flames but was unable to do so and died as a result.

This explanation certainly did not satisfy Larry Arnold, who had taken a particular interest in the subject of human spontaneous combustion. He went to Coudersport to investigate, and felt that he found many oddities about the case.

One of the oddest things was the death certificate, which listed as cause of death "Asphyxiation and 90 percent burning of body." How, Arnold wondered, could the conclusion of asphyxiation have been arrived at when only part of one leg and a pile of ashes remained? "Of course, 'burning of the body' contributed to the death, but what caused the terribly hot flames which were the ultimate cause of death?" Arnold asks.

The major puzzle, according to Arnold, was how Dr. Bentley's body could have been burned so completely without burning down the rest of the house, or at least causing a lot more damage. Arnold says that the body must have been consumed in a 'heat that could not be matched even in a crematorium. Despite the popular conception that cremation reduces a body to a handful of ashes, there are invariably recognizable bone fragments mixed with the ashes.

Arnold believes that Dr. Bentley's fiery death was probably due to human spontaneous combustion. He also believes that a number of similar modern cases can also be found. Rather than attributing the burning to the humors of the body, as was done in Victorian times, Arnold holds that there is a correlation between periods of "severe magnetic flux" and mysterious fires.

"This raises the fascinating prospect of interrelations between human, terrestrial, and possibly cosmic energy patterns," he writes.

In addition to Arnold, who must be regarded as

the chief current apostle of human spontaneous combustion, many other Forteans have shown an interest in the subject. Charles Fort himself had references to it scattered throughout his books. Fort constantly expressed surprise that the subject has not attracted more attention.

Ivan Sanderson listed forty-one separate cases of human spontaneous combustion, and cited many more in which animals inexplicably burst into flame.

What Sanderson regarded as the best case took place in St. Petersburg, Florida, in July 1951. A Mrs. Hardy Reeser, a sixty-seven-year-old widow, was burned up under mysterious circumstances. The armchair in which she had been sitting and an end table were also burned, but nearby papers and drapes and other highly flammable materials in the room were undamaged. All that was left of Mrs. Reeser were a few small pieces of charred backbone, her strangely shrunken skull, and an undamaged left foot. In life Mrs. Reeser had weighed 175 pounds. Her charred remains weighed less than ten.

Of all the explanations offered in such cases certainly the weirdest was put forward by Fortean Ronald J. Willis of the International Fortean Organization (INFO). Willis suggested that there might be some sort of strange "fire beings which swoop down on certain individuals and incinerate them mysteriously. . . . What possible motivation these creatures

Mrs. Reeser's room after the fire (St. Petersburg *Times & Evening Independent*).

could have is beyond our imagination, but then much of the Universe is still beyond our ken. It's not a pleasant thing to think about when going to bed late tonight!"

I'm not sure Charles Dickens would have accepted such an explanation. But he would have been deeply gratified by continuing interest in the subject of human spontaneous combustion.

7

THE PERSISTENT
PLESIOSAUR

In mid 1977 newspapers all over the world printed stories of how a Japanese fishing boat had hauled up a decaying "sea monster" off the coast of New Zealand.

Many of the newspaper accounts also carried a quote from Professor Yoshinori Imaizuni, director of research at the Tokyo National Science Museum. "It's not a fish, whale, or any other mammal. It's a reptile and the sketch looks very like a plesiosaurus. . . . This was a precious and important discovery for human beings. It seems to show that these animals are not extinct after all. It's impossible for only one to have survived."

So it seems that everybody's favorite candidate for underwater monster, the ancient plesiosaurus, has surfaced once again. But first let's briefly lay out the details of the case at hand.

Remains of a "sea monster" netted by a Japanese fishing boat off the coast of New Zealand (*UPI*).

Artist's conception of the plesiosaur (*The British Museum*).

On April 10, 1977, the crew of the Japanese fishing vessel *Zulyo Maru* pulled up its net from a 1,000-foot depth. To their surprise the fishermen found that the net contained about two tons of rotting something that looked like nothing they had ever seen before. Whatever it was had a small head, long neck, long tail, and four flippers. The total length was somewhat over thirty feet. It was also so badly decayed that the rotting flesh was literally falling off the bones, and the mass dripped a fatty white ooze on the deck. It also stank horribly.

The *Zulyo Maru* was already carrying a large cargo of fish, and the crewmen were afraid that the decaying thing might contaminate the valuable cargo. So they threw it overboard.

It was one of those moments that turn monster buffs prematurely gray. So many times in the past when it seemed as though we were within inches of finally getting solid evidence to the identity of one of the huge unknown sea creatures that have been reported so often, some careless crewman tosses it overboard, or people leave it on the beach and it gets washed out to sea, or it is otherwise lost, and we are left with only verbal accounts that are tantalizing but not very nourishing.

Now it seemed the same thing had happened once again. But in this case at least, the destruction of evidence was not quite complete. Michihiko Yano, a fishery company executive on board the *Zulyo Maru*, took four color photographs and made a couple of sketches before the thing was thrown overboard. Apparently some samples of the creature's flesh were also salvaged, though accounts vary as to how much. Some reports say flesh and bones, while others speak of a relatively small "whisker-like" specimen of flesh only.

The photographs that were published along with the story show a mass that is roughly plesiosaur in shape. But they are not clear enough for us to draw any definite conclusions. Michihiko Yano's sketches, however, make the creature look very definitely like a plesiosaur. The dimensions on the sketches are: overall length about 33 feet; tail about 6½ feet; the neck about 5 feet; and the small head about 1½ feet. They are perfect plesiosaur measurements.

The plesiosaur is one of a large number of gigantic marine reptiles that lived during the era of the dinosaurs. They were not seagoing dinosaurs *per se*, for the term dinosaur is properly applied only to the land-living reptiles. But the dinosaurs and the plesiosaurs may have been closely related. As far as we can judge from fossil remains the plesiosaurs were quite successful and numerous. Still they died off suddenly and rather mysteriously, along with all the other giant marine reptiles and the dinosaurs themselves, about seventy million years ago.

Could some of these creatures possibly have survived until the present era? The conventional scientific answer to that question is absolutely not. There is not a single bit of solid evidence that the plesiosaur or any of the other giant reptiles of that era survived. Yet from time to time over the centuries, people have reported seeing huge unknown creatures in the sea and even in bodies of fresh water. Many of these creatures appear to resemble a plesiosaur more than they do anything else.

Probably the most famous monster in the entire world, the Loch Ness monster, has usually been reported as looking like a plesiosaur. The best picture of Nessie, the London surgeon's photograph taken in 1934, shows what might be the long neck and small head of a plesiosaur. An underwater photograph taken in 1972 shows dimly what appears to be a flipper, which might belong to a plesiosaur and a 1975 underwater photo dimly shows what might be a long-necked creature. Practically everyone who has ever tried to construct a composite picture of the Loch Ness monster has come up with something that looks like a plesiosaur.

To contend that a herd of dinosaurs has somehow survived undetected on the earth's surface is to stretch credulity too far. The earth's surface is reasonably well explored. But to say that a herd of huge marine reptiles has survived undetected in the depths of the ocean or in some deep, dark lake like Loch Ness, well, that is not quite so absurd.

So the thing pulled up off the coast of New Zealand could have been a plesiosaur. Could have been, but, alas for romance, it probably wasn't. Other scientists who looked at the information from Japan came up with different candidates to account for the rotting remains. One said it might be a leatherback turtle. (Not a good suggestion, for though the leatherback is a seagoing creature and the largest member of the turtle family, the largest specimen is only nine feet.) Dr. Carl Hubbs of the La Jolla, California, Scripps Institution of Oceanography, suggested "probably a small whale . . . so rotten that most of the flesh was sloughed off." Possible, but there is an even better candidate—a shark.

Professor Fujio Yasuda of Tokyo Fisheries University said that an examination of the tissue specimen from the thing showed that it contained various amino acids that are seen in sharks and that the chemical composition was nearly identical to that of a shark. Fortean Hal R. Aldrich, reviewing the case for the journal of the International Fortean Organization, protests that sharks don't grow as large as this thing was. But they do, and larger. The carcass measured about thirty-three feet. The confirmed size record for the peaceable, plankton-eating whale shark is fifty-nine feet, and they may well get much larger. Even the man-eating white shark—the hero of *Jaws*—has been known to exceed forty feet in length. But the most probable candidate is another plankton-eating shark called the basking shark.

These sharks also reach a length of over forty feet,

and their rotted carcasses have probably provoked more plesiosaur rumors than any other single object. There is an anatomical peculiarity about the basking shark—its most shark-like feature—its jaws are not firmly attached to its backbone. As a result, when a shark begins to rot, its entire jaw structure may fall away, leaving only the small cranium and what looks like a long neck. The bottom half of the tail is also not directly attached to the backbone, and it, too, can fall away, giving the remains the appearance of a long tapering tail rather than a two-lobed tail.

Another possible clue can be found in the "whisker-like" appearance attributed to the tissue samples. When a shark begins to rot, its muscles will break up into individual whisker-like fibers.

It is no longer possible to prove that the rotting carcass the Japanese fishermen tossed back into the sea was a large shark. But the evidence certainly points strongly in that direction. Several other "plesiosaurs" which were not thrown back did indeed turn out to be sharks.

But let us not leave the subject of plesiosaur survival on so downbeat a note. There has been one fairly recent development which should go a long way toward keeping the plesiosaur survival theory popular.

One of the primary objections to identifying the

Loch Ness monster as a plesiosaur was that the waters of the loch were too cold to support a large reptile. Reptiles are cold-blooded and couldn't live in the chilly waters of the loch.

The cold-water problem has sent monster buffs scurrying about looking for other possible candidates for the Loch Ness monster. They have come up with long-necked seals, giant eels, even monstrous sea worms. But most will admit to a private longing for the old plesiosaur identification.

The same objection has also been raised to the identification of the sea monster as a plesiosaur. The creature has often been sighted in cold northern seas, where a reptile could not survive.

A primary reason why the plesiosaur theory looked so good for the Japanese fishermen's monster was that the thing was hauled up in warm waters. According to wire service reports Tokio Shikama, identified as "a scholar of ancient animals" at Yokohama National University, said: "It has to be a plesiosaur. These creatures must still roam the seas off New Zealand feeding on fish." He called the area an "ideal habitat," abounding in fish and with a surface temperature of about 50° F.

But would a plesiosaur really need warm water? Was it really a cold-blooded reptile at all? Over the past few years scientists have begun to re-evaluate their data on dinosaurs. The once unanimous assumption that dinosaurs were slow-moving cold-blooded reptiles has begun to crumble. A considerable body of evidence has now been amassed to indicate that the dinosaurs were warm-blooded, and thus could tolerate far greater temperature ranges than modern reptiles can. Indeed, many scientists are now convinced that the dinosaurs were not reptiles at all, but belong in a separate classification altogether. They also think that dinosaurs were the direct ancestors of modern birds. It seems that our whole view of ancient animals has been a rather narrow one. If the dinosaurs were warm-blooded, why not the plesiosaur as well? And that would get rid of the cold-weather and -water objections to its identification as a variety of water monsters.

That is, I grant you, taking a very long speculative leap. But that's the fun of mysteries of this type. So it may turn out to be Plessie, rather than Nessie. Now all that remains is the little matter of catching one.

8

MOON MADNESS

Even a man who is pure in heart
And says his prayers by night
Can become a wolf when the wolfbane blooms
And the autumn moon is bright.

That bit of Hollywood poetry comes from the famous film *The Wolf Man*. In that film, and practically every other werewolf movie ever made, the moon is considered the element that triggers the transformation from man to wolf.

In werewolf films there is at least one scene, and usually more than one, in which we are given a shot of the full moon, and then we watch the werewolf change from his human form by growing hair and fangs before our very eyes.

The full moon (*Lick Observatory*).

A madman thinking himself to be a wolf devours his victims (*Engraving by Lucas Cranach*).

People have believed in werewolves for centuries. But until quite recently there was little to connect the werewolf with the full moon. Generally the werewolf transformation was supposed to be brought

THE MOON.

The moon as shown
on a tarot card.

about by any one of a large number of magical means. I have never been able to discover just when the werewolf and the moon were first connected. But the connection is an entirely logical, even inevitable, one.

The werewolf did not necessarily have to grow hair and fangs. A person possessed by a sudden frenzy to go running about on all fours, making animal noises, and perhaps attacking people and animals and tearing at them with his teeth and nails might be considered a werewolf. Today such a person would immediately be classed as a madman, not a werewolf. The possible connection between madness and the moon is an extremely ancient one, and one that may not be as silly as it first sounds.

Primitive peoples simply assumed that the moon had magical qualities. More civilized peoples have believed that the moon had definite effects upon the body, and most especially upon the mind. Our word lunatic, from the word luna, or moon, reflects the belief that a man's mind could be affected by the moon.

Through the centuries references to moon madness abound in both learned and popular sources. A fifth-century Greek medical treatise states, "As often as one is seized with terror and fright and madness during the night and leaps up from his couch and rushes out of doors he is said to be suffering from the visitations of the moon."

The church fathers recognized no influences other than God and the Devil. St. Jerome, who lived in the fifth century of the Christian era, tried to turn the old moon-madness belief around and give it an orthodox Christian interpretation. "Lunatics are not really smitten by the moon, but are believed to be so, through the subtlety of demons who by observing the seasons of the moon strive to bring an evil report against the creature, that it might redound to the blasphemy of the Creator." The Devil's servants, in Jerome's opinion were simply using the moon as a cover for their own purposes.

The Church issued similar warnings throughout the centuries, but the belief in moon madness had too great a hold on the popular imagination for the warnings to do much to end the belief. Though astrology had also been repeatedly condemned by the Church, it, too, remained popular and thus reinforced the idea that the heavenly bodies could directly affect human behavior.

Paracelsus, a sixteenth-century physician and alchemist, was one of the most eccentric geniuses in the history of science. He broke with many of the erroneous medical practices that had been handed down without change since the days of the early Greeks. For this reason he can be regarded as a genuine pioneer of science. Yet much of his own theory was based on astrology and magical principles. He was half scientist, half magician, but he was extremely influential. Much of his writing is obscure, but on the subject of moon madness he was unusually clear.

He divided mental illness into four classes, one of which were the *Lunatici*, "those who get the disease from the moon and react according to it."

Les lupins, werewolf-like creatures from French folklore, were said to appear only on moonlit nights.

Paracelsus believed that in susceptible individuals the moon had the ability to "tear reason out of man's head by depriving him of humors and cerebral virtues." Magnetism was also important in Paracelsus' view, and he compared the moon's ability to pull reason from the mind to a magnet's ability to attract iron. This "power of attraction," he said, "is at its height during the full moon, and therefore it attracts more strongly and the lunatics suffer most then."

Later and much more orthodox physicians continued to believe that the moon had an effect on the mind. Dr. John Hunter wrote in 1834, "Mad people are certainly more affected at particular periods of the moon than at other times. The full of the moon has the greatest effect . . . it not only affects those who have a natural predisposition but also some who have injuries done to the brain by external violence."

But by the time Hunter wrote this, the once universal belief that there was such a thing as moon madness was under serious attack in the scientific community. Dr. Benjamin Rush, a signer of the Declaration of Independence and premier physician of the young republic, came down firmly on both sides of the controversy. He believed that the full moon did indeed have an effect upon the behavior of mental patients, but it was simply the light of the moon, not some mysterious astrological or magnetic influence that created the disturbances.

Even that modest opinion was soon displaced by total skepticism. Today most medical researchers would say that the moon has no effect upon the mental state whatsoever and that the idea of moon madness is an old wives' tale. Most would say that, but not all. Ideas held for centuries are not got rid of that easily.

The belief that the moon caused certain people to go mad was based on the impression of individual observers. Today we have broad-based statistical studies that are supposed to give us a truer picture. The trouble is that statistical studies often contradict one another. No single study, or even group of studies, can be said to "prove" anything. But still they can be intriguing. A couple of studies conducted over the last thirty years hint that, perhaps, the old moon-madness idea isn't just superstition after all.

A study made at the Eastern State Hospital at Williamsburg, Virginia, indicated that there were more admissions of mental patients to the hospital during the new and full moon than at any other period during the lunar cycle.

A study done in the 1960s at an Ohio hospital also showed what the investigators termed a "significantly" higher number of admissions to the psychiatric ward during the new- and full-moon phases than any other. In Texas, Dr. A. D. Pokorny came to a similar conclusion after surveying the statistics on admissions to mental hospitals throughout the state.

Admissions to mental hospitals aren't the only intriguing numbers in the study of moon madness. In 1972 two Florida researchers, Drs. A. L. Lieber and C. R. Sherin, reported that out of a total of 1,949 murders committed in Dade County, Florida, over the period of 1956–70, a significantly higher percentage was committed when there was a full moon.

This study seemed to confirm what some law-enforcement officers already suspected, that the moon does have an effect on crime. In 1961 Wilfred Faust of the Philadelphia Police Department said, "The seventy-odd policemen who deal with telephone complaints have always reported that activity, especially crimes against the person, seemed to increase as the night of the full moon drew near. People whose antisocial behavior had psychotic roots—such as firebugs, kleptomaniacs, destructive drivers, and homicidal alcoholics—seemed to go on a rampage as the moon rounded, calming down as the moon waned."

A past chief of New York City's Bureau of Fire Investigation believed that on nights of the full moon there were going to be more fires due to arson than at any other time of the month.

Suicide is yet another violent human activity which has sometimes been linked to the phases of the moon. Dr. D. Lester of the Buffalo, New York, Suicide Prevention and Crisis Center said that his figures for the years 1964–68 show that in four of those five years there were more successful suicides around the full moon than at any other time. Dr. S. A. Levinson, the chief coroner of Chicago, found the same sort of correlation in a study done of suicides in that city. A

Canadian and an Australian study both found that there was a significantly larger number of suicides and suicide attempts among women during the period of the full moon.

One can take such reports and draw the sweeping conclusion: "Science proves that the full moon drives people mad." Such a conclusion would be totally un-scientific. Each year uncounted thousands of scientific papers are published in journals throughout the world. If you look hard enough and long enough you can probably find research to support practically any position, no matter how absurd. Some papers report faulty, incomplete, or misinterpreted research. It is important that any piece of research be confirmed again and again and again by different investigators. That is one of the reasons why the Nobel Prize Committee usually waits for years after a discovery before conferring a prize upon the discoverers. The discovery may turn out to be wrong. In fact, the Nobel Committee once did give out an award for a discovery that later turned out to be wrong.

So the position in regard to moon madness is this: There are a few studies which seem to show a cor-relation between the full moon and various types of mental disturbance. But the bulk of the scientific studies of mental illness, murder, and suicide show no such correlation. As I said, the positive studies represent a hint that the old idea of moon madness may not be only a superstition after all, but they are only a hint.

It's an even longer jump from statistical analyses of hospital admissions and suicides to werewolves and the full moon. But if, when the moon is full, you get a sudden urge to howl and run around on all fours— watch it!

9

---◆---

LEVITATION

In June 1977 the transcendental meditation movement surprised just about everyone with the an-
nouncement that people could be taught how to levitate. The TM movement founded by the Maharishi
Mahesh Yogi had gained a measure of scientific respectability with the claim that their system of meditation could promote a deep and healthful relaxation.
For a while the TM movement was growing at an
enormous rate. However, starting in about 1975,
growth of TM slowed down, at least in part because
of competition from rival relaxation techniques that
were both cheaper and less shrouded in mystery and
ritual.

The levitation claim seemed so far out, so startling, that it threatened to shatter what scientific respectability remained to TM. Orthodox science absolutely denies the possibility of levitation. TM leaders were rather cagey about giving public demonstrations of this power of levitation, but some outsiders were allowed to witness the feat. I have not seen TM levitation myself, but I have talked to someone whose opinion and knowledge in such matters I respect who did witness such a demonstration. He says that what appeared to be going on was that the TMers had learned to hop from a cross-legged lotus position. This is an extremely difficult acrobatic feat. It is not the sort of thing that you or I could do without a great deal of practice. (Indeed I would have to do a great deal of practicing in order to be able to *hold* the lotus position for any length of time.) Still such a feat, if my informant's explanation is correct, is not levitation as that word is generally meant. We think of levitation as something supernatural or paranormal, an act that transcends the known laws of physics. If my friend's analysis of TM levitation is correct, the act is no more supernatural than the feats of a Nadia Comaneci on the uneven parallel bars, and probably a great deal less difficult.

Yet it is not altogether surprising that TM, which is at least a semi-religious movement, should become

The British medium Colin Evans did public demonstrations of levitation during the 1930s. This is an infra-red photograph taken in the dark during a séance. It is suspected that Evans simply jumped and was snapped during his leap (*New York Public Library*).

involved with levitation. Holiness and the ability to transcend gravity by levitation have frequently been linked. This isn't only true in the "mysterious East" either. In the Middle Ages tales of the ability to levitate and actually fly considerable distances were almost routinely told about Christian holy men, despite occasional warnings from church authorities about excessive credulity in such matters.

Most of the stories about flying saints are hopelessly vague and hence uncheckable. None of them would pass muster as courtroom testimony. They are even less adequate when tested by the much more rigorous demands of scientific inquiry. But the tales are so persistent and widespread that they are at least intriguing.

The feats of levitation attributed to St. Joseph of Copertino, a seventeenth-century Italian monk, are among the most amply documented, and the most startling. St. Joseph, according to these accounts, was a rather simple ascetic, who often fell into ecstatic raptures. Sometimes while in these mystic states his body rose from the ground.

One of the saint's more impressive feats was reported to have taken place during the visit of a Spanish nobleman and his wife. The nobleman's wife and her retinue of women expressed the strong wish to see the famous friar. But Joseph didn't like the

St. Joseph of Copertino, a seventeenth-century monk, who was said to levitate and even to fly (*New York Public Library*).

idea, since he avoided all possible contact with women. However, his superior insisted that he visit the women in the church. Joseph said he would do so, but did not know if he would be able to speak. So grudgingly the friar left his cell and entered the church full of women. The first object Joseph saw was a statue of the Immaculate Conception. Upon seeing this Joseph uttered a cry, rose into the air, and flew over the statue. There he remained for some time in a state of speechless adoration. Then he uttered another shriek, flew back to the door, bowed to the Mother of God, kissed the ground, and, with his head inclined and cowl lowered, hastened back to his cell. Behind him he left a group of ladies fainting with amazement over what they had just witnessed.

As I said, such tales of Christian holy men were not unusual a few hundred years ago. Over the last few centuries the number of accounts of flying saints has dropped off considerably. Indeed, if such tales were told today they would probably be viewed with deep suspicion even by the devout, who might at least admit the possibility that such things could happen.

In the East, tales of flying holy men have been more numerous and more persistent. In fact, in some traditions the ability to levitate appears to have been considered commonplace and relatively unimportant. There is a tale concerning the Buddha, who was sitting with a group of disciples discussing spiritual development when a stranger entered the room. The stranger asked if he might become one of the disciples. As proof of his worthiness, the stranger sat down in the lotus position, slowly rose a few feet off the ground, then proceeded to circle the room several times. The Buddha watched the performance without interest. When it was over he told his disciples that they should not be distracted by such displays but should turn their attention to the more important matter of inner spiritual development.

It is perhaps understandable that the Buddha could be so blasé. But most of us could hardly watch such a performance without a consuming interest. We would like to know if it can be done without tricks.

Probably the largest number of reasonably recent levitation accounts come from nineteenth- and early twentieth-century India. British officials and travelers were always sending back descriptions of the "Indian rope trick." In this a rope would be tossed up in the air and held there by an unknown force. Then someone, usually a boy, climbed up the rope. In some accounts the boy disappeared at the top. More common, and seemingly more authentic, are accounts of "ordinary" levitations. In these the person sits, or lies down on the ground, then seems to lift off and hover with no visible means of support. The observers were often amazed and thought the Indians had some sort of supernatural powers.

But such accounts must be treated with considerable caution. Most of those whom the British saw "levitating" in Indian market places or at public celebrations were professional performers. They were not holy men. The British often could not tell the difference or did not care. The performers were not necessarily any more "holy" than Western stage magicians, nor were they necessarily any less skillful at creating an illusion.

I have seen a number of "levitations" performed by magicians. The most impressive are the ones in which the magician appears to levitate an assistant. At the climax of the performances the assistant seems to be suspended rigidly about four feet above the ground. The magician then passes a metal hoop over the levitated assistant from head to foot to show that there are no supporting wires or bars. It is an amazing illusion. But I have been assured by professional magicians that it is only an illusion, there is nothing supernatural about it. I don't know how it is done, I can't even begin to conceive how it is done, and the magicians won't tell. Magicians are very secretive. They have to be. If we knew how the tricks were done we would not pay to see them.

Some Forteans think that more than trickery may be involved in the Indian levitations. R. J. M. Rickard, editor of the British publication *Fortean Times*, reviewed accounts of levitation and found them so intriguing that he wrote an article on them, saying, "I welcome this opportunity to rescue them from obscurity."

Rickard then goes on to quote a number of nineteenth-century accounts, mostly from India. One of the most interesting was one by Harry Kellar, who according to Rickard "was familiar with every trick in the (Western) magician's repertoire." The feat took place during the visit of the Prince of Wales to India in the winter of 1875–76. It was part of a performance given in the Great Plaza of Calcutta before the prince and fifty thousand other spectators:

"After a salaam to the Prince, the old fakir (a word originally meaning a poor man and not a faker) took three swords with straight crossbarred hilts, and buried them hilt downwards about six inches in the ground. The points of these swords were very sharp as I afterwards informed myself. A younger fakir stretched himself upon the ground at full length . . . and after a pass or two [by] the hands of the old man, appeared to become rigid and lifeless."

An assistant then came forward, and both taking hold of the head and feet of the young man "laid the stiffened body upon the points of the swords, which appeared to support it without penetrating the flesh. The point of one sword was immediately under the nape of the neck, that of the second rested midway between his shoulders, and that of the third [at] the base of the spine; there was nothing under his legs. . . . The boy tipped neither to the right nor the left, but seemed to be balanced with mathematical accuracy."

Rickard then goes on to summarize the rest of Kellar's report:

"After the third man retired to the side, the master took out a dagger and dug away the soil from the hilt of the first sword, and removed it—the body remained motionless. The second and third swords were likewise taken from under the body, which, there in broad daylight and under the eyes of all the spectators, preserved its horizontal position without visible support, about 2 feet from the ground. After a while the fakir summoned his assistant and holding each end of his stiff body gently lowered their companion to the ground, where, after a few more passes, he was animated once more. Kellar says he could devise an illusion of this feat (given a closed room, devices, and an audience facing one direction)—but not in broad daylight on unprepared ground and surrounded in the open by witnesses. Naturally this does not mean it definitely was not an illusion, but if it was then it deserves study in itself as a remarkable phenomenon."

Rickard cites a number of other accounts including a 1936 levitation by one Subbayah Pullavar, which was minutely photographed and described by P. T. Plunkett:

"Everything was now ready. Subbayah Pullavar marked out a circle close around the tent, under which he was going to levitate, by pouring water onto the floor of the hot and dusty compound [and instructed] that nobody with leather-soled shoes was to go inside it. When Subbayah's assistant told us it was time for the tent to be removed we took up positions [on opposite sides] just outside the ring and photographed every position from every angle."

The photographs which are very clear show Subbayah Pullavar hovering horizontally in the air with no visible means of support, except that his hand is resting on a stick, wrapped in cloth, that touches the ground at an angle. According to the written account he maintained this position for about four minutes. It is, of course, possible that the performer was actually balancing his body in the air by means of the stick. One of the hallmarks of a great acrobat is that he can do things that look supernatural to the untrained. This feat certainly does.

While the Indian and medieval Christian levitations are the best known, there have been many others. During the late nineteenth and early twentieth centuries when belief in spiritualism was at its height many spirit mediums claimed to be able to levitate during séances. The greatest of the nineteenth-century mediums, the Scotsman D. D. Home, was reported to have floated out of one window and in through another, in the presence of several witnesses.

The nineteenth-century medium D. D. Home was said to be able to levitate during séances (*New York Public Library*).

There are also several photographs of mediums levitating during séances, though these are a good deal less impressive than the photos of Subbayah Pullavar. The mediums seem to be jumping rather than floating.

This catalogue of levitations could be extended almost indefinitely. Some reference to the ability to levitate can be found in virtually every culture, from every period in history. Not only have there been levitations of people reported, but levitations of objects as well. There are persistent tales that the pyramids of Egypt, the monuments of the Incas, or Stonehenge were constructed with the aid of levitation. The logic behind such claims is that there is no other way by which the gigantic stones used in the construction could have been moved by people who possessed only the most primitive technology. There are tales of the Druids riding about on levitated stones, and misty accounts that even today, in remote monasteries there are holy men who can levitate huge stones simply by "chanting."

Orthodox science naturally scoffs at such claims. All reported feats of levitation are put down to tricks, illusions, or misreporting. Scientists quite justifiably point out that no one has ever been able to levitate so much as a feather under laboratory conditions.

Forteans just as naturally reject such negative conclusions. "Personally," says Rickard, "I'm inclined to accept for now that levitations do occur, and that we are very likely dealing with a natural process which can be affected spontaneously, or through an act of will. . . ."

10

---◆---

THINGS FROM THE SKY

You have undoubtedly heard the expression that it is "raining cats and dogs."

Brewer's Dictionary of Fact and Fable informs us that:

"In northern mythology the cat is supposed to have great influence on the weather and 'The cat has a gale of wind in her tail' is a seafarer's expression when a cat is unusually frisky. Witches that rode on storms were said to assume the form of cats. The dog is a signal of wind, like the wolf, both of which were attendants of Odin, the storm god.

"Thus the cat may be taken as a symbol of the down-pouring rain, and the dog of the strong gusts of wind accompanying a rain storm."

I have never heard of a case in which cats and/or dogs actually did rain down from the sky, but I would not be surprised if the account of such an event exists somewhere. Practically everything else— frogs, fish, blocks of ice, seeds, pieces of tinfoil "angel hair," etc., etc.—has at one time or another been reported as falling mysteriously from the sky.

The subject absolutely fascinated Charles Fort, who collected an enormous number of references to things falling from the sky.

In his *The Book of the Damned* (and by damned Fort meant excluded by orthodox science) he started out with falling frogs. Fort had a distinctly odd, roundabout writing style. Sometimes it was a little difficult to figure out what he was driving at. Here are a few of the things he had to say about falling frogs:

"Tremendous number of little toads, one or two months old, that were seen to fall from a great thick cloud that appeared suddenly in a sky that had been cloudless, August 1804, near Toulouse, France, according to a letter from Prof. Pontus to M. Arago.

"Many instances of frogs that were seen to fall

A nineteenth-century engraving of a fall of fish.

from the sky. (*Notes and Queries* 8–6–104); accounts of such falls, signed by witnesses.

"*Scientific American*, July 12, 1873:

"A shower of frogs which darkened the air and covered the ground for a long distance is reported as the result of a recent rainstorm in Kansas City, Mo."

Frog falls, however, are not nearly as numerous as fish falls. The sixteenth-century Swedish ecclesiastic and writer Olaus Magnus told of such events in his massive history of Scandinavia.

The March 1972 issue of *Australian Natural History* lists fifty-four separate falls of fish (and a few of frogs) recorded in Australia between 1879 and 1971. Australia is not particularly noted for its rains of fish, it is merely that someone bothered to collect all the accounts and list them in chronological order. They make interesting reading. In February of 1909 a man named T. Iredale reported that small fishes had rattled down on his tin roof during a storm. According to the *Australian Museum Magazine* hundreds of little fish called gudgeons were found in the streets after a rain at Gulargambone, New South Wales. The Sydney *Morning Herald* reported that on July 17, 1959, hundreds of fishes about four inches long fell in Lismore, New South Wales.

Probably the best known of the fish falls was the one that occurred at Mountain Ash in the valley of

Aberdare, Glamorganshire, Wales, on February 11, 1859.

A man named John Lewis was standing out in the rain when fish began to pour down over him. One slipped down the neck of his shirt, and several got caught in his hatbrim. The fall went on for only about two minutes, then it stopped, and ten minutes later started again for another two minutes. The fish fell over a very limited area, about 80 yards by 12 yards. These fish were not only fresh, they were very lively. A few samples were sent, still alive, to the British Museum for examination. Authorities there determined that there were two types, minnows and sticklebacks. Later the fish that survived were reportedly exhibited at the Zoological Garden in Regent's Park. They may have been the only famous minnows in history.

Scientists at the British Museum were inclined to dismiss the Mountain Ash incident as some sort of joke. Perhaps someone had thrown a bucketful of fish over Mr. Lewis.

A secondary explanation, and one that is most commonly raised to explain falls of fish and frogs, is a whirlwind. This mass of rapidly swirling air sucks up the creatures from lakes and ponds and deposits them elsewhere, like the cyclone that transported Dorothy to Oz, except not as violent.

Forteans naturally scoff at such mundane explanations. They raise objections too numerous and often too technical to be explained in any detail here. Suffice it to say that their objections are valid if the events surrounding the fish and frog falls are reported accurately. That, however, is a very big if indeed, for there is an irresistible tendency to make an event sound more wonderful than it really was.

But to proceed. Fort had collected a few records of snake falls, not great crowds of snakes—that would be rather alarming—but just one snake at a time, or at the most just a few. Fort said he had a letter from a Miss Margaret McDonald, of Hathorne, Massachusetts, stating that a number of speckled snakes fell in the streets of Hathorne after a thunderstorm.

On May 26, 1920, what was identified as a poisonous snake from Egypt fell into a garden in central London. On the next three days poisonous adders fell, or rather appeared, in various parts of London.

Commented Fort, "Common sense tells me that probably some especially vicious joker had been scattering venomous snakes around. But some more common sense tells me that I cannot depend upon common sense."

During July of 1822 great quantities of seeds of unknown origin fell in various parts of Germany.

The peasants who were often short of food tried to boil the seeds into an edible condition, but boiling seemed to soften them not in the slightest.

Another vegetable substance that has occasionally been reported falling from the sky is straw or hay. A great quantity of it was reported to have fallen on London's Heathrow airport on August 10, 1972.

Then there is the problem of "angel hair." Angel hair is a sort of general term that Forteans use to describe a variety of filamentous or stringy material that is supposed to fall from the sky or otherwise appear mysteriously on the ground. A material made of thin glass fiber and called angel hair was once used to decorate Christmas trees. It was determined to be a dangerous substance and has not been sold for some time. However, I believe that this is where Forteans picked up the term angel hair.

According to one of America's most prominent and prolific Forteans, the late Ivan Sanderson, "The published literature of so-called angel hair is massive. It crops up in heavy scientific journals, and from way back in the nineteenth century. Even modern meteorological publications mention it from time to time. . . ."

Generally angel hair seems to disintegrate when it has lain on the ground for a short time, so there have been few samples to examine.

Closely akin to angel hair is a ribbon-like metallic substance that looks like cut-up aluminum foil and has been reported fairly often. Ufologists—those people who are interested in UFOs and generally believe that they are spaceships from other planets—insist that this sort of stuff often falls after a UFO has passed overhead.

Ice from the sky is another Fortean favorite. Now we all know that ice can fall from the sky in the form of hail. In violent thunderstorms hailstones several inches in diameter have been known to fall. But what is one to say about what happened at a place called Ord, Scotland, on the estate of a Mr. Moffat in August of 1847? There, a gigantic piece of ice nearly twenty feet around fell near the farmhouse. According to a contemporary account, "It had a beautiful crystalline appearance, being nearly all quite transparent. . . . It was principally composed of small squares, diamond-shaped, of from 1 to 3 inches in size, all firmly congealed together." The ice chunk melted before anyone could weigh it, but the writer observed that it was a good thing that it didn't fall on Moffat's house, because it would have crushed the inhabitants.

On October 16, 1960, in Melbourne, Australia, a couple of lumps of ice the size of footballs fell from a cloudless sky onto a golf course, narrowly missing some golfers, according to an AP story.

In addition there are reported falls of stones, and ashes, and unidentifiable gooey stuff, and all sorts of other things that have been lovingly collected and listed by Forteans.

What does it all mean? The conventional answer to that question is that it does not mean a great deal, or, more accurately, it all probably means a great number of different things. Different falls can be explained in different ways, and we are not dealing with a single phenomenon.

But Charles Fort and his disciples think differently. Their great passion is to find an underlying unity in all these strange events. Fort hinted (he rarely said anything directly) that all of these "things from the sky" came from somewhere else, perhaps another universe.

Ivan Sanderson said it more directly. "These things," he wrote, "don't really fall out of the sky (like rain or airplanes) but they 'come through' from one or more other 'universes.' They have been appearing since ever, *and they must come from somewhere*."

You may make of such an opinion whatever you wish.

BIBLIOGRAPHY

General

Fort, Charles. *The Books of Charles Fort*. New York:
    Henry Holt, 1941.
Godwin, John. *Unsolved: The World of the Unknown*.
    Garden City, N.Y.: Doubleday, 1976.
Sanderson, Ivan. *Investigating the Unexplained*. Englewood
    Cliffs, N.J.: Prentice-Hall, 1972.

Chapter 1

Baxter, John, and Atkins, Thomas. *The Fire Came By*.
    Garden City, N.Y.: Doubleday, 1976.
Cohen, Daniel. *How the World Will End*. New York:
    McGraw-Hill, 1973.

Bibliography

Chapter 2

Phantom Butchers. *The INFO Journal*. Vol. 4, No. 2, 1974.

Saunders, David, and Harkins, Roger. *UFOs? Yes!*. New York: New American Library, 1968.

Stewart, James R. "Cattle Mutilations." *The Zetetic*. Vol. 1, No. 2, 1977.

Chapter 3

Corliss, William R. (compiler) *Strange Planet, A Sourcebook of Unusual Geological Facts*. Glen Arm, Md.: The Sourcebook Project, 1975.

Martin, P. S., and Wright, H. E. (editors). *Pleistocene Extinctions, The Search for a Cause*. New Haven, Conn.: Yale University Press, 1967.

Chapter 4

De Camp, L. Sprague, and De Camp, Catherine. *Ancient Ruins and Archaeology*. New York: Doubleday, 1964.

Donnelly, Ignatius. *Atlantis: the Antediluvian World* (revised). N.Y.: Gramercy, 1949.

Heuvelmans, Bernard. *On the Track of Unknown Animals*. New York: Hill & Wang, 1959.

Chapter 5

Reed, Graham. *The Psychology of Anomalous Experience*. Boston: Houghton Mifflin, 1974.

Bibliography

Chapter 6

Arnold, Larry E. "Fire Leynes." *Fortean Times*. No. 22, Summer 1977.

———. "The Flaming Fate of Dr. Bentley." *Fate*, April 1977.

Dickens, Charles. *The Annotated Christmas Carol*. New York: Clarkson N. Potter, 1976.

———. *Bleak House*. First published 1853. Many editions.

Gaddis, Vincent. *Mysterious Fires and Lights*. New York: McKay, 1967.

Russell, Eric Frank. *Great World Mysteries*. New York: Mayflower-Dell, 1967.

Willis, Ronald J. "The Burning People." *The INFO Journal*. Vol. 2, No. 4, 1972.

Chapter 7

Aldrich, Hal R. "Was It a Plesiosaur?" *The INFO Journal*. Vol. 6, No. 3, 1977.

Desmond, Adrian J. *The Hot-Blooded Dinosaur*. New York: Dial, 1976.

Heuvelmans, Bernard. *In the Wake of the Sea Serpents*. New York: Hill & Wang, 1968.

Chapter 8

Abel, E. L. *Moon Madness*. New York: Fawcett, 1976.

Chapter 9

Dingwall, Eric J. *Some Human Oddities*. London: Home & Van Thale, 1947.

Rickard, R. J. M. "Walking, Sitting and Lying on Air." *Fortean Times*. No. 21, Spring 1977.

Bibliography

Chapter 10

Bayless, Raymond. *Experiences of a Psychical Researcher*. New York: University Books, 1972.

"Falls: Fishes, Ice, Straw." *The INFO Journal*. Vol. 3, No. 2, 1973.

Schadenwald, Robert. "Fish Falls and Whirlwinds." *Fortean Times*. No. 22, Summer 1977.

Willis, Ronald J. "Ice Falls." *The INFO Journal*. Vol. 1, No. 3, 1968.

INDEX

Index

Index

Index

DANIEL COHEN is a prolific free-lance writer with more than fifty books for adults and young people in print. Formerly managing editor of *Science Digest* magazine, he has also written extensively on the occult, the supernatural, and the bizarre. Among his books are *A Natural History of Unnatural Things; In Search of Ghosts; Magicians, Wizards, and Sorcerers; The Ancient Visitors; Monsters, Giants, and Little Men from Mars;* and *Ghostly Animals.* His articles have appeared in such magazines as *The Nation, Coronet,* and *Pageant.* Mr. Cohen, his wife, a writer of supernatural fiction, and their daughter share a house in Port Jervis, New York, with a large collection of cats and dogs.